Mifflin Harcourt

Math

Grade 2

Copyright © 2014 by Houghton Mifflin Harcourt Publishing Company

All rights reserved. No part of this work may be reproduced or transmitted in any form or by any means, electronic or mechanical, including photocopying or recording, or by any information storage or retrieval system, without the prior written permission of the copyright owner unless such copying is expressly permitted by federal copyright law.

Permission is hereby granted to individuals to photocopy entire pages from this publication in classroom quantities for instructional use and not for resale. Requests for information on other matters regarding duplication of this work should be addressed to Houghton Mifflin Harcourt Publishing Company, Attn: Contracts, Copyrights, and Licensing, 9400 Southpark Center Loop, Orlando, Florida 32819-8647.

Printed in the U.S.A.

ISBN 978-0-544-26820-3

5 6 7 8 9 10   2266   22 21 20 19 18 17

4500684224   B C D E F G

If you have received these materials as examination copies free of charge, Houghton Mifflin Harcourt Publishing Company retains title to the materials and they may not be resold. Resale of examination copies is strictly prohibited.

Possession of this publication in print format does not entitle users to convert this publication, or any portion of it, into electronic format.

Core Skills Math

GRADE 2

Table of Contents

© Houghton Mifflin Harcourt Publishing Company

Table of Contents
Core Skills Math, Grade 2

© Houghton Mifflin Harcourt Publishing Company

Table of Contents

Core Skills Math, Grade 2

© Houghton Mifflin Harcourt Publishing Company

Mathematics Correlation Chart

Skills	Page Numbers
Addition	1, 2, 3, 4, 5, 13, 14, 15, 16, 17, 18, 19, 25, 52, 53, 54, 55, 56, 57, 58, 59, 60, 61, 63, 64, 130, 131, 132, 133, 134, 135
Area	82, 83
Subtraction	6, 7, 8, 9, 10, 22, 65, 66, 67, 68, 69, 70, 71, 136, 137, 138, 139, 140
Addition and Subtraction Practice	24, 73, 101
Even and Odd Numbers	30, 31, 32
Fact Families	11, 20, 21, 23
Fractions	84, 85, 86, 87
Graphs and Charts	102, 103, 104, 105, 106, 107, 108, 109, 110, 111
Length	88, 89, 90, 91, 92, 93, 94, 95, 96, 97, 98, 99, 100
Money	33, 34, 35, 36, 37, 38, 39, 40, 41, 42, 43, 44, 45
Multiplication	141, 142, 143, 144, 145
Place Value	26, 27, 28, 29, 112, 113, 114, 115, 116, 117, 118, 119, 120, 121, 122, 123, 124, 125, 126, 127, 128, 129
Problem Solving	12, 62, 72, 74, 75, 76, 146
Shapes	77, 78, 79, 80, 81
Time	46, 47, 48, 49, 50, 51

© Houghton Mifflin Harcourt Publishing Company

Name _____ Date _____

Joining Groups

Use the pictures. Write the sums.

1.
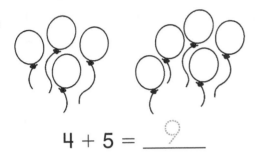

$4 + 5 =$ _____

2.

$7 + 1 =$ _____

3.

$3 + 6 =$ _____

4.

$2 + 6 =$ _____

5.

$5 + 2 =$ _____

6.

$3 + 5 =$ _____

7.

$4 + 2 =$ _____

8.

$1 + 5 =$ _____

NUMBER SENSE

9. Which pair has the greatest sum?
Circle the pair.

$9 + 3$ $\qquad$ $9 + 2$ $\qquad$ $9 + 5$ $\qquad$ $9 + 1$

1

© Houghton Mifflin Harcourt Publishing Company

Order and Zero Properties

Write the sums.

1.	0	8	4	6	9	1
	+ 8	+ 0	+ 6	+ 4	+ 1	+ 9
	8					

2.	5	3	7	0	2	8
	+ 3	+ 7	+ 6	+ 5	+ 6	+ 2

3.	6	9	3	0	5	9
	+ 0	+ 3	+ 6	+ 4	+ 4	+ 0

VISUAL THINKING

Circle the train that has the fewest cubes.

4.
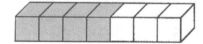

5.

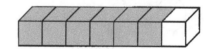

2

© Houghton Mifflin Harcourt Publishing Company

Adding on a Number Line

Draw lines to match.

1. (number line 0 to 10) $1 + 6 = 7$

2. (number line 0 to 10) $3 + 6 = 9$

3. (number line 0 to 10) $0 + 3 = 3$

4. (number line 0 to 10) $5 + 4 = 9$

5. (number line 0 to 10) $8 + 2 = 10$

6. (number line 0 to 10) $6 + 3 = 9$

STORY CORNER

7. Tell a story. Write an addition sentence.

_____ + _____ = _____

_____ children

3

© Houghton Mifflin Harcourt Publishing Company

Counting On

Count on to add.

1. 8   6   5   8   7   9
    + 2   + 1   + 2   + 3   + 1   + 2
   10

2. 9   5   6   4   7   8
    + 1   + 3   + 2   + 2   + 3   + 1

3. 3   3   2   9   8   4
    + 1   + 2   + 1   + 3   + 2   + 1

4. 3   5   4   3   7   6
    + 2   + 1   + 3   + 3   + 2   + 3

REASONING

Write the missing number.

5.

1 2 3 (5)

_____

6.

1 3 5 (9)

_____

4

© Houghton Mifflin Harcourt Publishing Company

Name _____   Date _____

More Counting On

Circle the greater number. Then count on to add.

1. 2   8   5   1   7   3
    +⑤   + 1   + 3   + 6   + 2   + 7
      7

2. 1   3   4   9   2   2
    + 4   + 4   + 2   + 1   + 6   + 8

3. 2   7   8   6   3   2
    + 9   + 1   + 3   + 3   + 5   + 4

4. 9   7   3   2   1   3
    + 3   + 3   + 6   + 8   + 5   + 1

| REASONING |

Write the missing number.

5.

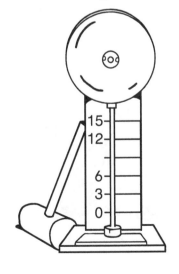

_____

6.

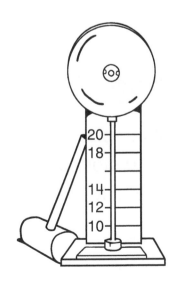

_____

© Houghton Mifflin Harcourt Publishing Company

Zeros in Subtraction

Subtract.

1. $3 - 3 =$ ___0___ $5 - 0 =$ _____ $4 - 4 =$ _____

2. $6 - 0 =$ _____ $7 - 7 =$ _____ $9 - 9 =$ _____

3. $4 - 0 =$ _____ $6 - 6 =$ _____ $8 - 0 =$ _____

4. $8 - 8 =$ _____ $7 - 0 =$ _____ $1 - 0 =$ _____

5.
$$
\begin{array}{r} 2 \\ -\,2 \\ \hline \end{array}
\qquad
\begin{array}{r} 3 \\ -\,0 \\ \hline \end{array}
\qquad
\begin{array}{r} 1 \\ -\,1 \\ \hline \end{array}
\qquad
\begin{array}{r} 9 \\ -\,0 \\ \hline \end{array}
\qquad
\begin{array}{r} 5 \\ -\,5 \\ \hline \end{array}
$$

STORY CORNER

6. Look at the picture.
   Make up a story problem.
   Ask a friend to solve it.

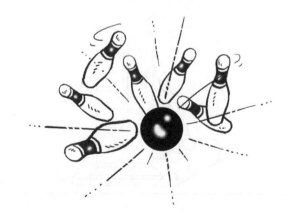

 _____ ◯ _____ = _____

© Houghton Mifflin Harcourt Publishing Company

Subtracting on a Number Line

Write the number sentence that the number line shows.

1.

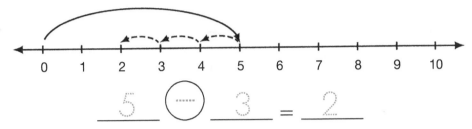

____5____ ⊖ ____3____ = ____2____

2.

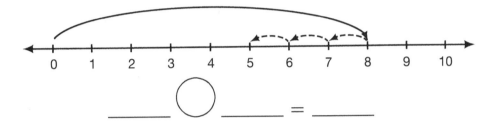

_____ ◯ _____ = _____

3.

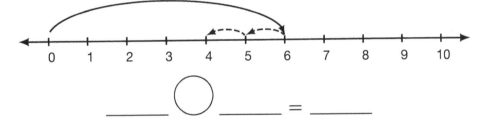

_____ ◯ _____ = _____

4.

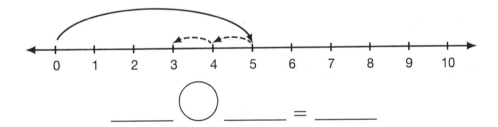

_____ ◯ _____ = _____

VISUAL THINKING

5. Circle the number line that shows subtraction.

7

© Houghton Mifflin Harcourt Publishing Company

Name _____   Date _____

Counting Back

Subtract.

1. 6   (6, 5, 4)   9   5   3   10
   − 2   − 2   − 1   − 1   − 2
    4

2. 7   4   8   2   10   5
   − 1   − 2   − 2   − 1   − 1   − 2

3. 8   7   9   3   6   4
   − 1   − 2   − 1   − 2   − 1   − 1

PROBLEM SOLVING

Write a number sentence to solve.

4. Lou wins 4 bears.
   He gives 2 away.
   How many bears does
   he have left?

   ____ ◯ ____ = ____

   ____ bears

5. Sara sees 6 rabbits.
   Then 1 runs away.
   How many rabbits
   are left?

   ____ ◯ ____ = ____

   ____ rabbits

8

© Houghton Mifflin Harcourt Publishing Company

Name _____ Date _____

More Counting Back

Count back to subtract.

1. Say 10. 9, 8

$10 - 2 = \underline{}$

2. Say 8. 7, 6, 5

$8 - 3 = \underline{}$

3. Say 9. 8, 7, 6

$9 - 3 = \underline{}$

4. Say 8. 7

$8 - 1 = \underline{}$

5.
$$\begin{array}{cccccc}
9 & 9 & 10 & 8 & 9 & 10 \\
-2 & -1 & -3 & -2 & -3 & -1 \\
\hline
\end{array}$$

NUMBER SENSE

Use a calculator. Write the answer.

6. ON/C 6 − 2 − 2 − 2 = _____

7. ON/C 8 − 2 − 2 − 2 − 2 = _____

© Houghton Mifflin Harcourt Publishing Company

Name _____ Date _____

Counting Up

Circle the number that is less. Then count up to find the difference.

1. $\begin{array}{r} 4 \\ -2 \\ \hline 2 \end{array}$
    $\begin{array}{r} 3 \\ -2 \\ \hline \end{array}$
    $\begin{array}{r} 10 \\ -9 \\ \hline \end{array}$
    $\begin{array}{r} 5 \\ -2 \\ \hline \end{array}$
    $\begin{array}{r} 7 \\ -5 \\ \hline \end{array}$
    $\begin{array}{r} 4 \\ -3 \\ \hline \end{array}$

2. $\begin{array}{r} 9 \\ -6 \\ \hline \end{array}$
    $\begin{array}{r} 8 \\ -7 \\ \hline \end{array}$
    $\begin{array}{r} 6 \\ -4 \\ \hline \end{array}$
    $\begin{array}{r} 7 \\ -4 \\ \hline \end{array}$
    $\begin{array}{r} 5 \\ -4 \\ \hline \end{array}$
    $\begin{array}{r} 8 \\ -5 \\ \hline \end{array}$

3. $\begin{array}{r} 5 \\ -3 \\ \hline \end{array}$
    $\begin{array}{r} 8 \\ -6 \\ \hline \end{array}$
    $\begin{array}{r} 9 \\ -8 \\ \hline \end{array}$
    $\begin{array}{r} 6 \\ -5 \\ \hline \end{array}$
    $\begin{array}{r} 10 \\ -7 \\ \hline \end{array}$
    $\begin{array}{r} 9 \\ -7 \\ \hline \end{array}$

4. $\begin{array}{r} 6 \\ -3 \\ \hline \end{array}$
    $\begin{array}{r} 7 \\ -6 \\ \hline \end{array}$
    $\begin{array}{r} 10 \\ -8 \\ \hline \end{array}$
    $\begin{array}{r} 4 \\ -2 \\ \hline \end{array}$
    $\begin{array}{r} 5 \\ -3 \\ \hline \end{array}$
    $\begin{array}{r} 9 \\ -6 \\ \hline \end{array}$

REASONING

Solve.

5. Dan has 10 cards.
   Dan has 1 more card than Becky.
   Becky has 1 more card than Ted.
   How many cards does Ted have?

_____ cards

10

© Houghton Mifflin Harcourt Publishing Company

Fact Families

Write the fact families.

1.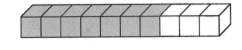

___ ◯ ___ ◯ ___

___ ◯ ___ ◯ ___

___ ◯ ___ ◯ ___

2.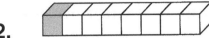

___ ◯ ___ ◯ ___

___ ◯ ___ ◯ ___

___ ◯ ___ ◯ ___

___ ◯ ___ ◯ ___

3.

___ ◯ ___ ◯ ___

___ ◯ ___ ◯ ___

___ ◯ ___ ◯ ___

___ ◯ ___ ◯ ___

4.

___ ◯ ___ ◯ ___

___ ◯ ___ ◯ ___

___ ◯ ___ ◯ ___

___ ◯ ___ ◯ ___

NUMBER SENSE

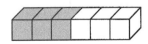

5. Look at the cube train.

How many facts are in this family? _____

© Houghton Mifflin Harcourt Publishing Company

Name _____ Date _____

Problem Solving

WRITE A NUMBER SENTENCE

Write a number sentence to solve.

1. Helen had 9 pennies.
   She gave away 2 of them.
   How many did she have left?

   _9_ (−) _2_ = _7_

   _7_ pennies

2. The vase has 5 flowers.
   The pot has 5 flowers.
   How many flowers are there?

   _____ ◯ _____ = _____

   _____ flowers

3. Lin buys 10 pears.
   She eats 4 of them.
   How many are left?

   _____ ◯ _____ = _____

   _____ pears

STORY CORNER

4. Tell a story. Write a number sentence.

   _____ ◯ _____ = _____

   _____ crayons

12

© Houghton Mifflin Harcourt Publishing Company

Name _____ Date _____

Doubles

Use counters. Write the sums.

$$\begin{array}{r} 3 \\ + 3 \\ \hline 6 \end{array}$$

$$\begin{array}{r} 6 \\ + 6 \\ \hline 12 \end{array}$$

1. $\begin{array}{r} 1 \\ + 1 \\ \hline \end{array}$ $\begin{array}{r} 7 \\ + 7 \\ \hline \end{array}$ $\begin{array}{r} 2 \\ + 2 \\ \hline \end{array}$ $\begin{array}{r} 8 \\ + 8 \\ \hline \end{array}$ $\begin{array}{r} 4 \\ + 4 \\ \hline \end{array}$

2. $\begin{array}{r} 0 \\ + 0 \\ \hline \end{array}$ $\begin{array}{r} 3 \\ + 3 \\ \hline \end{array}$ $\begin{array}{r} 6 \\ + 6 \\ \hline \end{array}$ $\begin{array}{r} 9 \\ + 9 \\ \hline \end{array}$ $\begin{array}{r} 5 \\ + 5 \\ \hline \end{array}$

Write the sums. Then circle doubles.

3. $\begin{array}{r} 3 \\ + 2 \\ \hline \end{array}$ $\begin{array}{r} 6 \\ + 4 \\ \hline \end{array}$ $\begin{array}{r} 4 \\ + 4 \\ \hline \end{array}$ $\begin{array}{r} 7 \\ + 2 \\ \hline \end{array}$ $\begin{array}{r} 3 \\ + 3 \\ \hline \end{array}$ $\begin{array}{r} 5 \\ + 5 \\ \hline \end{array}$

PROBLEM SOLVING

4. Tony found 2 shells. David found the same number. How many shells did the boys find in all?

_____ shells

5. Rosa saw 3 crabs in the sand. She saw the same number in the water. How many crabs did she see?

_____ crabs

© Houghton Mifflin Harcourt Publishing Company

Unit 2
Core Skills Math, Grade 2

Doubles Plus One

Circle the number in each pair that has the greater sum.
Then write the sum.

1. 4   (4)   3   3   6   5
   + 4   + 5   + 4   + 3   + 5   + 5
   ───── ─────   ───── ─────   ───── ─────
     8   9

2. 6   6   2   2   8   9
   + 7   + 6   + 2   + 3   + 8   + 8
   ───── ─────   ───── ─────   ───── ─────

Add.
Circle sums of doubles with ▮ blue ▷ **.**
Circle sums of doubles plus one with ▮ red ▷ **.**

3. 3   3   2   8   7   4
   + 4   + 3   + 2   + 7   + 6   + 4
   ─────   ─────   ─────   ─────   ─────   ─────
     7

VISUAL THINKING

4. Circle the pictures that show doubles plus one.

  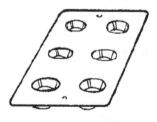 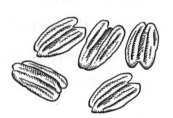

© Houghton Mifflin Harcourt Publishing Company

Adding 9

Add.

1.
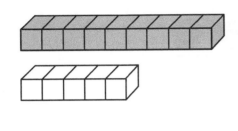

$\begin{array}{r} 9 \\ + 5 \\ \hline 14 \end{array}$

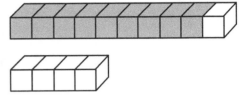

$\begin{array}{r} 10 \\ + 4 \\ \hline \end{array}$

2.
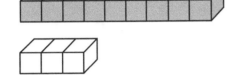

$\begin{array}{r} 9 \\ + 3 \\ \hline \end{array}$

$\begin{array}{r} 10 \\ + 2 \\ \hline \end{array}$

3.

$\begin{array}{r} 9 \\ + 8 \\ \hline \end{array}$

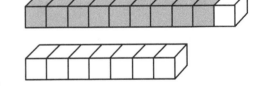

$\begin{array}{r} 10 \\ + 7 \\ \hline \end{array}$

4. $\begin{array}{r} 9 \\ + 4 \\ \hline \end{array}$ 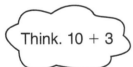 Think. 10 + 3 $\begin{array}{r} 9 \\ + 6 \\ \hline \end{array}$ $\begin{array}{r} 9 \\ + 7 \\ \hline \end{array}$ $\begin{array}{r} 8 \\ + 9 \\ \hline \end{array}$ $\begin{array}{r} 3 \\ + 9 \\ \hline \end{array}$

NUMBER SENSE

Circle the two that name the same number.

5. 9 + 2   10 + 3   10 + 1

6. 10 + 3   9 + 4   10 + 4

© Houghton Mifflin Harcourt Publishing Company

Name _____ Date _____

Make a 10

Use a 10-frame and counters. Find the sums.

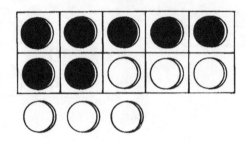

1. 7   9   5   4   9   8
   + 6   + 3   + 7   + 9   + 6   + 5
   13

2. 2   8   9   6   4   9
   + 9   + 6   + 5   + 9   + 7   + 4

3. 3   8   7   9   6   5
   + 8   + 4   + 5   + 7   + 8   + 9

| PROBLEM SOLVING |

Write a number sentence to solve.

4. Miko saw 7 seals. Soon 5 of
   them swam away. How many
   seals were left?

   _____ seals

5. Alice saw 6 baby seals and 7
   mother seals. How many seals
   did she see?

   _____ seals

16

Adding More Than Two Addends

**Sometimes, looking for a 10 or a double
makes adding easy. Add.**

1.

$\begin{array}{r} 2 \\ 2 \\ +\ 7 \\ \hline 11 \end{array}$ } 4

$\begin{array}{r} 2 \\ 6 \\ +\ 4 \end{array}$ } 10

$\begin{array}{r} 5 \\ 3 \\ +\ 3 \end{array}$ } 6

$\begin{array}{r} 4 \\ 4 \\ +\ 5 \end{array}$ } 8

$\begin{array}{r} 8 \\ 2 \\ 1 \\ +\ 3 \end{array}$ } 10

2.

$\begin{array}{r} 7 \\ 5 \\ +\ 5 \end{array}$

$\begin{array}{r} 8 \\ 2 \\ +\ 7 \end{array}$

$\begin{array}{r} 1 \\ 4 \\ 6 \\ +\ 3 \end{array}$

$\begin{array}{r} 1 \\ 8 \\ 4 \\ +\ 4 \end{array}$

$\begin{array}{r} 6 \\ 4 \\ 3 \\ +\ 2 \end{array}$

$\begin{array}{r} 3 \\ 3 \\ 6 \\ +\ 1 \end{array}$

3.

$\begin{array}{r} 6 \\ 3 \\ +\ 7 \end{array}$

$\begin{array}{r} 2 \\ 1 \\ 6 \\ +\ 6 \end{array}$

$\begin{array}{r} 4 \\ 5 \\ 5 \\ +\ 2 \end{array}$

$\begin{array}{r} 9 \\ 0 \\ 9 \\ +\ 1 \end{array}$

$\begin{array}{r} 0 \\ 8 \\ 2 \\ +\ 8 \end{array}$

$\begin{array}{r} 2 \\ 2 \\ 4 \\ +\ 6 \end{array}$

REASONING

**Find each sum in your head.
Circle the ones with a sum greater than 10.**

4. $4 + 1 + 1 + 1 + 6$

5. $2 + 1 + 1 + 2 + 1$

6. $1 + 1 + 1 + 3 + 7$

7. $5 + 1 + 1 + 5$

8. $1 + 1 + 1 + 1 + 1 + 1 + 1 + 1$

© Houghton Mifflin Harcourt Publishing Company

Name _____ Date _____

Sums to 14

Complete the addition sentences. They should total the number in the box.

1. | 14 |

$5 + \underline{} = \underline{}$

$6 + \underline{} = \underline{}$

$7 + \underline{} = \underline{}$

$\underline{} + \underline{} = \underline{}$

2. | 13 |

$4 + \underline{} = \underline{}$

$5 + \underline{} = \underline{}$

$6 + \underline{} = \underline{}$

$\underline{} + \underline{} = \underline{}$

3. | 12 |

$3 + \underline{} = \underline{}$

$4 + \underline{} = \underline{}$

$5 + \underline{} = \underline{}$

$\underline{} + \underline{} = \underline{}$

4. | 11 |

$2 + \underline{} = \underline{}$

$3 + \underline{} = \underline{}$

$4 + \underline{} = \underline{}$

$\underline{} + \underline{} = \underline{}$

REASONING

5. Continue the pattern.

| 7 + 7 | 6 + 7 | 5 + 7 | 4 + 7 | | |

© Houghton Mifflin Harcourt Publishing Company

Unit 2
Core Skills Math, Grade 2

Sums to 18

Add.

1.

8	7	5	9	9	6
+ 5	+ 7	+ 7	+ 4	+ 8	+ 6
13					

2.

6	4	8	5	6	7
+ 8	+ 7	+ 6	+ 9	+ 9	+ 6

3.

9	9	7	6	8	4
+ 3	+ 9	+ 4	+ 7	+ 8	+ 8

4.

9	2	3	6	7	5
+ 8	+ 9	+ 9	+ 5	+ 5	+ 6

PROBLEM SOLVING

Write a number sentence. Solve.

5. There were 11 birds in the air. Then 8 of the birds landed. How many birds were still in the air?

____ ◯ ____ = ____

____ birds

6. There were 5 pink birds and 8 white birds standing in the water. How many birds were in the water?

____ ◯ ____ = ____

____ birds

© Houghton Mifflin Harcourt Publishing Company

Unit 2
Core Skills Math, Grade 2

Using Doubles to Subtract

Add or subtract. Then match.

1. $6 + 6 = \underline{}$ $10 - 5 = \underline{}$

2. $5 + 5 = \underline{}$ $4 - 2 = \underline{}$

3. $9 + 9 = \underline{}$ $12 - 6 = \underline{}$

4. $2 + 2 = \underline{}$ $14 - 7 = \underline{}$

5. $3 + 3 = \underline{}$ $6 - 3 = \underline{}$

6. $7 + 7 = \underline{}$ $18 - 9 = \underline{}$

7. $4 + 4 = \underline{}$ $16 - 8 = \underline{}$

8. $8 + 8 = \underline{}$ $8 - 4 = \underline{}$

PROBLEM SOLVING

9. Leo put 6 orange fish and 6 black fish in the bowl. How many fish did Leo put in?

_____ fish

10. Leo had 12 fish in his bowl. Then he took out 6 fish to put in his tank. How many fish were left in the bowl?

_____ ◯ _____ = _____

_____ fish

© Houghton Mifflin Harcourt Publishing Company

Name _____ Date _____

Using Other Addition Facts to Subtract

Subtract. Then color.

Color Code	
Answer	**Color**
2	black
3	purple
4	blue
5	brown
6	yellow
7	red
8	green
9	orange

NUMBER SENSE

Do these in your head. Then write the sums and differences.

1. 9 + 4 = 13,

    so 13 − 4 = _____.

2. 13 − 9 = 4,

    so 4 + 9 = _____.

3. 6 + 7 = 13,

    so 13 − 7 = _____.

4. 13 − 6 = 7,

    so 7 + 6 = _____.

© Houghton Mifflin Harcourt Publishing Company

Unit 2
Core Skills Math, Grade 2

Related Addition and Subtraction Facts

Write the differences.

1.

Subtract 3.	
12	
10	
11	

Subtract 5.	
11	
14	
13	

Subtract 4.	
11	
13	
12	

Subtract 6.	
14	
12	
8	

2.

Subtract 8.	
16	
12	
14	

Subtract 9.	
10	
15	
18	

Subtract 7.	
13	
16	
9	

Subtract 5.	
14	
11	
13	

3.

Subtract 6.	
10	
15	
9	

Subtract 8.	
13	
11	
15	

Subtract 9.	
11	
17	
16	

Subtract 7.	
15	
14	
10	

PROBLEM SOLVING

Write a number sentence to solve.

4. There were 6 snails on the rock. There were 7 snails in the sand. How many snails were there?

____ ◯ ____ = ____

____ snails

5. Rico had 12 shells, but he gave 3 away. How many shells did he have left?

____ ◯ ____ = ____

____ shells

© Houghton Mifflin Harcourt Publishing Company

Unit 2
Core Skills Math, Grade 2

Name _____ Date _____

Fact Families

Complete each number sentence.
Which one does not belong to the fact family? Circle it.

1. 15 − ____7____ = 8

7 + 8 = _____

7 + 7 = _____

_____ − 8 = 7

_____ + 7 = 15

2. 7 + 9 = _____

_____ − 9 = 7

16 − _____ = 9

9 + _____ = 16

9 + 9 = _____

3. 9 + _____ = 17

8 + _____ = 17

_____ − 9 = 8

17 − 8 = _____

16 − 8 = _____

4. 15 − 9 = _____

14 − 8 = _____

6 + _____ = 14

_____ − 6 = 8

8 + 6 = _____

NUMBER SENSE

5. Write the fact family for 🪣 🪣 🪣 🪣 🪣 🪣 🪣 ■ ■ ■ ■ ■ ■ .

_____ + _____ = _____   _____ − _____ = _____

© Houghton Mifflin Harcourt Publishing Company

Unit 2
Core Skills Math, Grade 2

Name _____ Date _____

Using Addition and Subtraction

Add or subtract. Use your addition table if you need to.

1. 9 + 7 = __16__   16 − 7 = _____   7 + 9 = _____

2. 5 + 8 = _____   13 − 8 = _____   8 + 5 = _____

3. 6 + 5 = _____   11 − 5 = _____   5 + 6 = _____

4.
    7   18   4   9   11   14
  + 7   − 9   + 7   + 9   − 4   − 7
 ̄ ̄ ̄ ̄ ̄   ̄ ̄ ̄ ̄ ̄   ̄ ̄ ̄ ̄ ̄   ̄ ̄ ̄ ̄ ̄   ̄ ̄ ̄ ̄ ̄   ̄ ̄ ̄ ̄ ̄

5.
   15   12   8   7   13   4
  − 7   − 4   + 5   + 8   − 8   + 8
 ̄ ̄ ̄ ̄ ̄   ̄ ̄ ̄ ̄ ̄   ̄ ̄ ̄ ̄ ̄   ̄ ̄ ̄ ̄ ̄   ̄ ̄ ̄ ̄ ̄   ̄ ̄ ̄ ̄ ̄

PROBLEM SOLVING

Read each story. Then write the number sentence to solve.

6. There were 5 red pails and
5 yellow pails in the shop.
How many pails were there?

____ ◯ ____ = ____

_____ pails

7. There were 5 red beach balls
and 6 yellow balls in the shop.
How many balls were there?

____ ◯ ____ = ____

_____ balls

© Houghton Mifflin Harcourt Publishing Company

Unit 2
Core Skills Math, Grade 2

Understanding Regrouping

Work with a friend. Complete the table.

	Ones	Join. Write how many.	Can you make a ten? Circle Yes or No.	Trade. Write how many.
1.	8 7	15 ones	Yes No	1 ten 5 ones
2.	4 5	____ ones	Yes No	____ ten ____ ones
3.	9 4	____ ones	Yes No	____ ten ____ ones
4.	6 6	____ ones	Yes No	____ ten ____ ones

NUMBER SENSE

5. Circle the two that name the same number.

1 ten 3 ones   11 ones   13 ones   1 ten 0 ones

© Houghton Mifflin Harcourt Publishing Company

Tens and Ones

Circle groups of ten. Write how many tens and ones.
Then write how many in all.

1.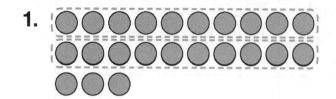

___2___ tens ___3___ ones ___23___

2.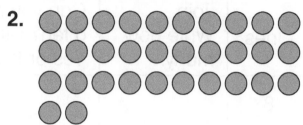

_____ tens _____ ones _____

3.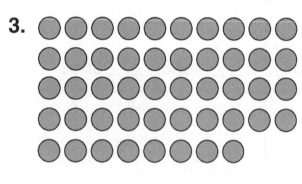

_____ tens _____ ones _____

4.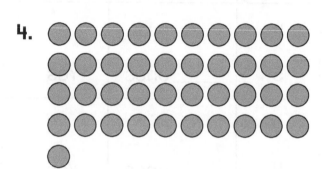

_____ tens _____ ones _____

5.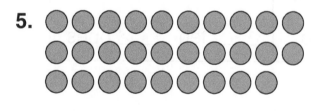

_____ tens _____ ones _____

6.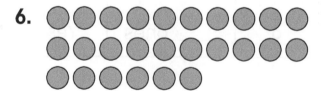

_____ tens _____ ones _____

VISUAL THINKING

7. Which is easier to count? Circle it. Tell why.

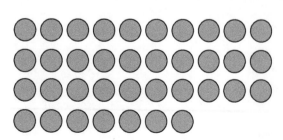 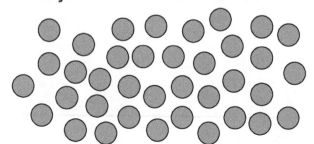

© Houghton Mifflin Harcourt Publishing Company

Unit 3
Core Skills Math, Grade 2

Name _____ Date _____

Tens and Ones to 50

Write the numbers.

1.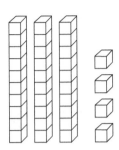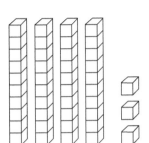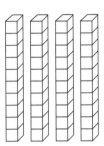

34 _____   _____   _____

Use tens and ones. Circle the number.

2. 3 tens 2 ones   1 ten 4 ones   4 ones

  32   23   41   14   40   4

3. 2 tens 1 one   2 tens 4 ones   3 tens

  21   12   42   24   30   3

NUMBER SENSE

Write the mystery numbers.

4. Emily's mystery number has a 2 in the tens place and a 5 in the ones place.

_____

5. Alonzo's mystery number has a 7 in the tens place and a 4 in the ones place.

_____

© Houghton Mifflin Harcourt Publishing Company

Unit 3
Core Skills Math, Grade 2

Name _____ Date _____

Tens and Ones to 100

Write the numbers.

1.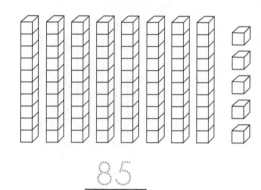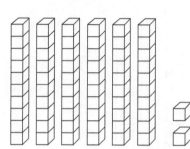

   _85_ _____

2. 8 tens   7 ones   _____   **3.** 6 tens   3 ones   _____

4. 5 tens   9 ones   _____   **5.** 8 tens   6 ones   _____

Circle the number.

6.   9 tens 2 ones   6 tens 5 ones   8 tens 3 ones
        92   29   65   56   38   83

7.   7 tens 6 ones   4 tens 8 ones   9 tens 3 ones
        67   76   48   84   39   93

VISUAL THINKING

8. **Look at the full jar of nuts. Circle the better estimate for the second jar.**

66

more than 30   fewer than 30

© Houghton Mifflin Harcourt Publishing Company

Different Ways to Write Numbers

Write the number another way.

1. 32

_____3_____ tens _____2_____ ones

2. forty-one

_____

3. 9 tens 5 ones

_____

4. 80 + 3

_____

5. 57

_____ tens _____ ones

6. seventy-two

_____ + _____

7. 60 + 4

_____

8. 4 tens 8 ones

_____

9. twenty-eight

_____ + _____

10. 80

_____ tens _____ ones

PROBLEM SOLVING

11. A number has the digit 3 in the ones place and the digit 4 in the tens place. Which of these is another way to write this number? Circle it.

3 + 4   40 + 3   30 + 4

© Houghton Mifflin Harcourt Publishing Company

Name _____ Date _____

Even and Odd Numbers

**Use cubes. Then color to show
each number. Circle even numbers.
Draw X on odd numbers.**

If you can make pairs, the number is even. If 1 cube is alone, the number is odd.

1. ⌇4⌇

2. 5

3. 1

4. 2

5. 11

6. 8
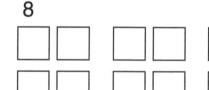

7. Use cubes. Circle the even numbers. Draw X on odd numbers.

    3   7   12   9   6   18   13   17   22

PROBLEM SOLVING

Add any two even numbers to solve. Circle the answer.

8. Even Number + Even Number = ?

           Even Number

           Odd Number

© Houghton Mifflin Harcourt Publishing Company

More Even and Odd Numbers

Color the ten frames to show the number. Circle <u>even</u> or <u>odd</u>.

1. 15
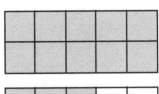
even   (odd)

2. 18
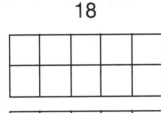
even   odd

3. 11
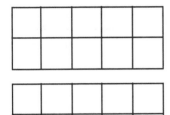
even   odd

4. 17
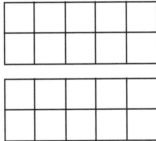
even   odd

5. 13
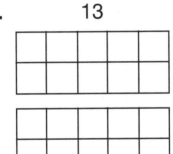
even   odd

6. 20
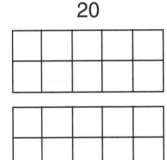
even   odd

PROBLEM SOLVING

7. Mr. Dell has an odd number of sheep and an even number of cows on his farm. Circle the choice that could tell about his farm.

9 sheep and 10 cows

10 sheep and 11 cows

8 sheep and 12 cows

© Houghton Mifflin Harcourt Publishing Company

Represent Even Numbers

Color the frames to show two equal groups for each number.
Complete the addition sentence to show the groups.

1.   8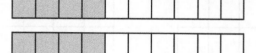

$\underline{8} = \underline{4} + \underline{4}$

2.   18

_____ = _____ + _____

3.   10

_____ = _____ + _____

4.   14

_____ = _____ + _____

5.   20

_____ = _____ + _____

6.   12

_____ = _____ + _____

PROBLEM SOLVING

Solve. Write or draw to explain.

7. The seats in a van are in pairs.
There are 16 seats. How many
pairs of seats are there?

_____ pairs of seats

© Houghton Mifflin Harcourt Publishing Company

Name _____ Date _____

Counting Pennies, Nickels, and Dimes

Count on to find the total amount.

1.

_5_ ¢ _10_ ¢ _15_ ¢ _16_ ¢   [16] ¢

2.

____ ¢ ____ ¢ ____ ¢ ____ ¢   [ ] ¢

3.

____ ¢ ____ ¢ ____ ¢ ____ ¢ ____ ¢   [ ] ¢

4.

____ ¢ ____ ¢ ____ ¢ ____ ¢ ____ ¢ ____ ¢   [ ] ¢

NUMBER SENSE

Use punch-out coins. Trace and write the value on each coin.

5. Use 3 coins to show 15¢.   6. Use 4 coins to show 40¢.

© Houghton Mifflin Harcourt Publishing Company

Unit 4
Core Skills Math, Grade 2

Name _____ Date _____

Quarter

Count on from 25¢. Write the total amount.

1.

   __25__ ¢ __35__ ¢ __40__ ¢ __41__ ¢   ¢

2.

   _____ ¢ _____ ¢ _____ ¢ _____ ¢ _____ ¢   ¢

3.

   _____ ¢ _____ ¢ _____ ¢ _____ ¢ _____ ¢   ¢

4.

   _____ ¢ _____ ¢ _____ ¢ _____ ¢ _____ ¢ _____ ¢   ¢

PROBLEM SOLVING

Use punch-out coins. Solve.

5. Phil has 1 quarter, 2 nickels, and 1 penny. How much money does Phil have?

   _____ ¢

6. Anna has 2 nickels. Sam has 3 pennies. How much more money does Anna have?

   _____ ¢ more

© Houghton Mifflin Harcourt Publishing Company

Unit 4
Core Skills Math, Grade 2

Comparing Money: Greatest Amount

Count on to find the total amounts. Circle the greatest amount.

1.

_31_ ¢   _25_ ¢   (_36_) ¢

2.

_____ ¢   _____ ¢   _____ ¢

3.

_____ ¢   _____ ¢   _____ ¢

| REASONING |

4. Len has 24¢.
Tina has 44¢.
Who can buy the toy?

_____

© Houghton Mifflin Harcourt Publishing Company

Name _____ Date _____

Make a Model

Write the amounts. You can use punch-out coins to help you.

1. Robert has 1 quarter, 1 dime, and 2 pennies. He spends 1 dime. How much money does he have now?

_27_ ¢

2. Nema has 5 nickels and 3 pennies. She spends 3 nickels. How much money does she have now?

_____ ¢

3. Julia has 2 dimes, 2 nickels, and 2 pennies. She spends 1 dime and 1 nickel. How much money does she have left?

_____ ¢

4. Greg has 1 quarter, 1 nickel, and 5 pennies. He finds 5 pennies. How much money does he have now?

_____ ¢

5. Harry has 6 nickels and 1 penny. He gives 3 nickels to a friend. How much money does he have now?

_____ ¢

6. Mae has 1 quarter and 4 nickels. She finds 1 dime. How much money does Mae have now?

_____ ¢

STORY CORNER

7. Look at the pictures. Make up a money story. Share it with a friend.

36

Name _____ Date _____

Combinations of Coins

Count on to find out how much money. Write the total amount.

1.

_72_ ¢

2.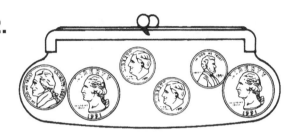

_____ ¢

3.

_____ ¢

4.

_____ ¢

5.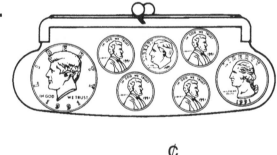

_____ ¢

6.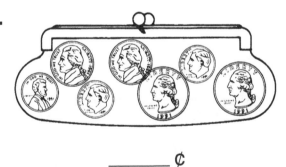

_____ ¢

REASONING

7. John has 67¢.

   Circle the belt that he can buy.

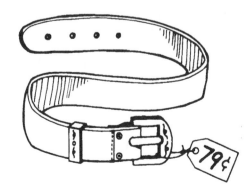

© Houghton Mifflin Harcourt Publishing Company

Unit 4
Core Skills Math, Grade 2

Exchanging Dimes for Pennies

Match.

1.

2.

3.

NUMBER SENSE

4. Circle the greater amount of money.

38

© Houghton Mifflin Harcourt Publishing Company

Name _____   Date _____

Equal Amounts

Work with a friend. Use your punch-out coins. Write the amount.
Work together to find fewer coins to make the same amount.
Draw. Write the value on each coin.

1.

_____55_____ ¢

2.

_____ ¢

3.

_____ ¢

NUMBER SENSE

4. Which amount could you make with the fewest coins?
   Use punch-out coins. Circle the amount.

   41¢   51¢   61¢

© Houghton Mifflin Harcourt Publishing Company

Dollar

**Work with a friend. Take turns showing ways
to make $1.00. Write how many.**

1. 1	1	0	0	25
2.				
3.				
4.				
5.				

NUMBER SENSE

6. Circle groups of coins that show the same amount of money.

© Houghton Mifflin Harcourt Publishing Company

Unit 4
Core Skills Math, Grade 2

Name _____ Date _____

Dollar and Cents

Circle how much money is needed.
Use punch-out money to help you.

1.

2.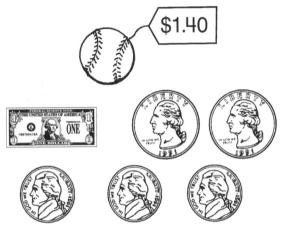

3.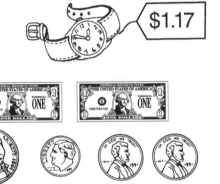

4.

PROBLEM SOLVING

5. Nick has 1 dollar and
3 nickels. Lola has 5 quarters.
Write how much each child has.
Then circle the greater amount.

Nick has _____.

Lola has _____.

6. Debra has  .
She wants
to buy 🦕 $1.30 .

Does she have enough money?
Circle **Yes** or **No**.

Yes   No

© Houghton Mifflin Harcourt Publishing Company

Name _____ Date _____

Counting Change

Work with a friend. Count up from the price to find the change.
Use punch-out coins to count out the change to your friend.

1. You have 70¢.
   You buy
   58¢

59¢ ___60___ ¢ ___70___ ¢

You have ___12___ ¢ change.

2. You have 35¢.
   You buy
   28¢

29¢ _____ ¢ _____ ¢

You have _____ ¢ change.

3. You have 65¢.
   You buy
   52¢

53¢ _____ ¢ _____ ¢ _____ ¢

You have _____ ¢ change.

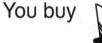
NUMBER SENSE

Solve. Use punch-out coins.
Trace and write the value on each coin.

4. Janine has 50¢ to spend. She buys a pin for 24¢.
   Use the fewest coins possible to show Janine's change.

© Houghton Mifflin Harcourt Publishing Company

Unit 4
Core Skills Math, Grade 2

Name _____ Date _____

Make a Decision

1. You have   .   _95_ ¢

Do you have enough money to buy a  ?   (Yes)   No

---

2. You have   .   _____ ¢

Do you have enough money to buy a  ?   Yes   No

---

3. You have   .   _____ ¢

Do you have enough money to buy a  ?   Yes   No

---

4. You have   .   _____ ¢

Do you have enough money to buy a  ?   Yes   No

---

NUMBER SENSE

5. Circle the better estimate.

more than 50¢

less than 50¢

© Houghton Mifflin Harcourt Publishing Company

Unit 4
Core Skills Math, Grade 2

Name _____ Date _____

Adding Money

Puzzle Sale

50¢

25¢

30¢

55¢

Use the pictures. Solve. Show your work.

1. Kim bought a giraffe puzzle and an elephant puzzle. How much did she spend?

_30_ ¢ + _50_ ¢ = _80_ ¢

_80_ ¢

2. Ms. Tuma bought 2 rhino puzzles. She used quarters. How much did she spend?

_____ ¢ + _____ ¢ = _____ ¢

_____ ¢

Circle the answer.

3. Carlos spent more than 50¢ on one puzzle. Which puzzle did he buy?

rhino   giraffe   elephant   cube

NUMBER SENSE

Circle Yes or No.

4. Mark has 75¢. He wants to buy a cube puzzle and a rhino puzzle. Does he have enough money?

Yes   No

© Houghton Mifflin Harcourt Publishing Company

Unit 4
Core Skills Math, Grade 2

Problem Solving

ADDING AND SUBTRACTING MONEY

Use punch-out coins. Add or subtract to solve.

1. Yolanda has 75¢. She buys a goldfish for 2 quarters. How much money does she have left?

_75_ ¢ − _50_ ¢ = _25_ ¢

_25_ ¢

2. Rita buys orange juice for 5 dimes and grape juice for 40¢. How much more does the orange juice cost than the grape juice?

_____ ¢ − _____ ¢ = _____ ¢

_____ ¢

3. Joel buys a pen for 32¢ and a pencil for a nickel. How much money does he spend?

_____ ¢ + _____ ¢ = _____ ¢

_____ ¢

4. Rob has 1 quarter and 2 pennies. He wants to buy a book that costs 37¢. How much more money does he need?

_____ ¢ − _____ ¢ = _____ ¢

_____ ¢

STORY CORNER

Work with a friend.

5. Make up two word problems about buying things. Have your friend write a number sentence for each of your word problems.

_____ ◯ _____ = _____   _____ ◯ _____ = _____

© Houghton Mifflin Harcourt Publishing Company

Name _____ Date _____

Time to the Hour and Half Hour

Look at the clock hands. Write the time.

1.

3:00

2.

3.

4.

5.

6.

PROBLEM SOLVING

7. Amy's music lesson begins at 4:00.
Draw hands on the clock to show this time.

46

© Houghton Mifflin Harcourt Publishing Company

15 Minutes: Quarter Hour

Write the times.

1.

| 5:15 |

2.

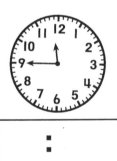

3.

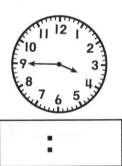

PROBLEM SOLVING

Use a punch-out clock. Write the times.

4. It is 8:30. What time will it be in 15 minutes?

____:____

5. It is 2:15. What time will it be in 15 minutes?

____:____

47

© Houghton Mifflin Harcourt Publishing Company

Name _____ Date _____

Time to 5 Minutes

Look at the clock hands. Write the time.

1.

8:15

2.

3.

4.

5.

6.

PROBLEM SOLVING

Draw the minute hand to show the time. Then write the time.

7. My hour hand points between the 4 and the 5. My minute hand points to the 9. What time do I show?

48

© Houghton Mifflin Harcourt Publishing Company

Problem Solving

DRAW A PICTURE

The magic hen will lay 1 egg every 5 minutes.
Draw the eggs that will be in the nest at each time.

1.   10:05   10:10   10:15   10:20

2.   10:25   10:30   10:35   10:40

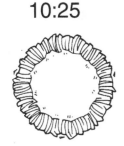      

3.   10:45   10:50   10:55   11:00

VISUAL THINKING

4. Circle the glass that has been on
   the table for 45 minutes.

49

© Houghton Mifflin Harcourt Publishing Company

Practice Telling Time

Draw the minute hand to show the time. Write the time.

1. quarter past 7

2. half past 3

3. 50 minutes after 1

4. quarter past 11

5. 15 minutes after 8

6. 5 minutes after 6

PROBLEM SOLVING

Draw hands on the clock to solve.

7. Josh got to school at half past 8.
   Show this time on the clock.

© Houghton Mifflin Harcourt Publishing Company

A.M. and P.M.

Write the time. Then circle A.M. or P.M.

1. walk the dog

A.M.

(P.M.)

4:40

2. finish breakfast

A.M.

P.M.

3. put on pajamas

A.M.

P.M.

4. read a bedtime story

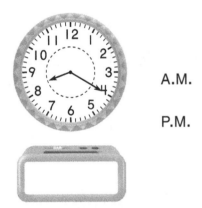

A.M.

P.M.

PROBLEM SOLVING

Use the list of times. Complete the story.

5. Jess woke up at _____. She got on

the bus at _____ and went to school.

She left school at _____.

> 3:15 P.M.
>
> 8:30 A.M.
>
> 7:00 A.M.

© Houghton Mifflin Harcourt Publishing Company

Name _____ Date _____

Regrouping

Put in tens and ones to show each problem.
Complete the table.

	Show	Join the ones. Write how many.	Can you make a ten? Circle Yes or No.	Trade. Write how many.
1.	13 + 8	__11__ ones	(Yes) No	__2__ tens __1__ ones
2.	35 + 7	_____ ones	Yes No	_____ tens _____ ones
3.	68 + 1	_____ ones	Yes No	_____ tens _____ ones
4.	29 + 9	_____ ones	Yes No	_____ tens _____ ones
5.	46 + 7	_____ ones	Yes No	_____ tens _____ ones

VISUAL THINKING

6. Write how many.

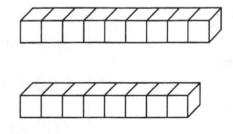

_____ cubes

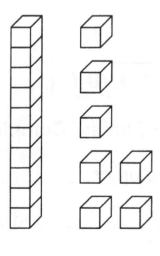

_____ cubes

© Houghton Mifflin Harcourt Publishing Company

Use Compensation

Show how to make one addend the next tens number.
Complete the new addition sentence.

1. 15 + 37 = ?  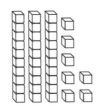 ___12___ + ___40___ = ___52___

2. 22 + 49 = ? 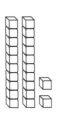 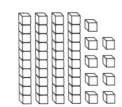 _____ + _____ = _____

3. 38 + 26 = ? 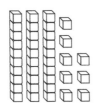 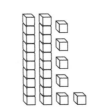 _____ + _____ = _____

4. 27 + 47 = ? 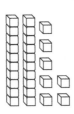 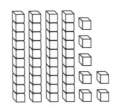 _____ + _____ = _____

PROBLEM SOLVING

Solve. Write or draw to explain.

5. The oak tree at the school was 34 feet tall.
Then it grew 18 feet taller.
How tall is the oak tree now?

_____ feet tall

© Houghton Mifflin Harcourt Publishing Company

Model Regrouping for Addition

Draw to show the regrouping. Write how many tens and ones in the sum. Write the sum.

1. Add 63 and 9.

Tens	Ones

__7__ tens __2__ ones

__72__

2. Add 25 and 58.

Tens	Ones

_____ tens _____ ones

_____

3. Add 58 and 18.

Tens	Ones

_____ tens _____ ones

_____

4. Add 64 and 26.

Tens	Ones

_____ tens _____ ones

_____

5. Add 17 and 77.

Tens	Ones

_____ tens _____ ones

_____

6. Add 16 and 39.

Tens	Ones

_____ tens _____ ones

_____

PROBLEM SOLVING

Choose a way to solve. Write or draw to explain.

7. Cathy has 43 leaves in her collection. Jane has 38 leaves. How many leaves do the two children have?

_____ leaves

© Houghton Mifflin Harcourt Publishing Company

Break Apart Addends as Tens and Ones

Break apart the addends to find the sum.

1. $\begin{array}{r} 18 \\ +21 \end{array}$ → $\underline{10}$ + $\underline{8}$

→ $\underline{20}$ + $\underline{1}$

$\underline{30}$ + $\underline{9}$ = $\underline{39}$

2. $\begin{array}{r} 33 \\ +49 \end{array}$ → _____ + _____

→ _____ + _____

_____ + _____ = _____

3. $\begin{array}{r} 72 \\ +18 \end{array}$ → _____ + _____

→ _____ + _____

_____ + _____ = _____

PROBLEM SOLVING

Choose a way to solve. Write or draw to explain.

4. Christopher has 28 baseball cards.
Justin has 18 baseball cards. How
many baseball cards do they have in all?   _____ baseball cards

© Houghton Mifflin Harcourt Publishing Company

Model and Record 2-Digit Addition

Draw quick pictures to help you solve. Write the sum.

1.

Tens	Ones
1	
3	8
+ 1	7
5	5

Tens	Ones

2.

Tens	Ones
5	8
+ 2	6

Tens	Ones

3.

Tens	Ones
4	2
+ 3	7

Tens	Ones

4.

Tens	Ones
5	3
+ 3	8

Tens	Ones

PROBLEM SOLVING

Choose a way to solve. Write or draw to explain.

5. There were 37 children at the park on
Saturday and 25 children at the park
on Sunday. How many children were
at the park on those two days?

_____ children

© Houghton Mifflin Harcourt Publishing Company

Understanding 2-Digit Addition

Add. Trade if you need to.

1.

tens	ones
¹ 2	5
+	8
3	3

tens	ones
4	3
+	7

tens	ones
2	1
+	2

tens	ones
2	8
+	2

2.

tens	ones
2	9
+	2

tens	ones
5	6
+	6

tens	ones
2	3
+	8

tens	ones
6	5
+	9

3.

tens	ones
4	5
+	8

tens	ones
3	3
+	9

tens	ones
5	7
+	5

tens	ones
3	0
+	4

NUMBER SENSE

Circle the better estimate.

4. 50 + 30 = 80, so 42 + 28 is   greater than 80.   less than 80.

5. 50 + 30 = 80, so 50 + 35 is   greater than 80.   less than 80.

57

© Houghton Mifflin Harcourt Publishing Company

Adding 2-Digit Numbers

Add. Trade if you need to.

1.

tens	ones
1	
4	2
+ 1	9
6	1

tens	ones
2	9
+ 1	7

tens	ones
4	7
+ 2	9

tens	ones
5	8
+ 1	6

2.

tens	ones
2	7
+ 1	9

tens	ones
1	9
+ 3	2

tens	ones
	5
+ 4	8

tens	ones
2	2
+ 3	8

PROBLEM SOLVING

Solve.

3. Cal had 29 cubes. He got 15 more cubes to model addition. Then how many cubes did Cal have?

4. Wendy had 4 tens and 2 ones. Then she got 3 more tens and 9 more ones. She traded some ones for a ten. Then how many tens and ones did she have?

_____ cubes

_____ tens and _____ ones

© Houghton Mifflin Harcourt Publishing Company

Name _____ Date _____

More Adding 2-Digit Numbers

Find the sum.

1.
```
  1
  38        55        23        29        24        19
+ 38      + 21      + 45      + 44      + 47      + 28
 76
```

2.
```
  84        82        12        37        78        54
+ 15      + 14      + 28      + 25      + 19      + 27
```

3.
```
  68        67        19        26        73        86
+  8      + 13      +  3      + 19      + 10      +  7
```

PROBLEM SOLVING

Circle the answer.

4. Theo had 5 tens and 15 ones. He traded 10 ones for a ten.
   Shari had 5 tens and 12 ones. She traded 10 ones for a ten.
   After that, who had more ones?

                    Theo   Shari

59

Name _____ Date _____

Addition Practice

Add.

1.
$$\begin{array}{r} \overset{1}{1}9 \\ +\ 28 \\ \hline 47 \end{array}$$
$$\begin{array}{r} 57 \\ +\ 26 \\ \hline \end{array}$$
$$\begin{array}{r} 78 \\ +\ 7 \\ \hline \end{array}$$
$$\begin{array}{r} 62 \\ +\ 17 \\ \hline \end{array}$$
$$\begin{array}{r} 47 \\ +\ 16 \\ \hline \end{array}$$
$$\begin{array}{r} 28 \\ +\ 37 \\ \hline \end{array}$$

2.
$$\begin{array}{r} 29 \\ +\ 23 \\ \hline \end{array}$$
$$\begin{array}{r} 17 \\ +\ 27 \\ \hline \end{array}$$
$$\begin{array}{r} 6 \\ +\ 76 \\ \hline \end{array}$$
$$\begin{array}{r} 68 \\ +\ 8 \\ \hline \end{array}$$
$$\begin{array}{r} 24 \\ +\ 27 \\ \hline \end{array}$$
$$\begin{array}{r} 55 \\ +\ 4 \\ \hline \end{array}$$

3.
$$\begin{array}{r} 37 \\ +\ 25 \\ \hline \end{array}$$
$$\begin{array}{r} 58 \\ +\ 4 \\ \hline \end{array}$$
$$\begin{array}{r} 19 \\ +\ 36 \\ \hline \end{array}$$
$$\begin{array}{r} 36 \\ +\ 35 \\ \hline \end{array}$$
$$\begin{array}{r} 18 \\ +\ 66 \\ \hline \end{array}$$
$$\begin{array}{r} 36 \\ +\ 57 \\ \hline \end{array}$$

PROBLEM SOLVING

Solve.

4. Arturo earned 16 points during his turn in a word game. He already had 39 points. What was his total score?

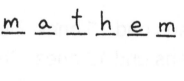

$$\begin{array}{r} \underline{\hspace{2cm}} \\ +\ \underline{\hspace{2cm}} \\ \hline \underline{\hspace{2cm}} \end{array}$$

_____ points

60

© Houghton Mifflin Harcourt Publishing Company

Name _____ Date _____

Finding Reasonable Sums

Circle the best estimate.

1. Kenny has 39 cards. Kate has 24 cards. About how many cards do they have?

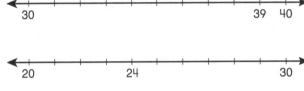

about 40   (about 60)   about 80

2. Beth has 43 cards. Jack has 37 cards. About how many cards do they have?

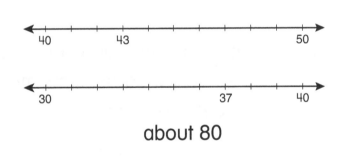

about 50   about 60   about 80

3. Terry has 52 cards. Elena has 19 cards. About how many cards do they have?

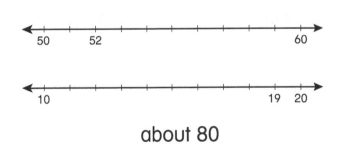

about 60   about 70   about 80

| NUMBER SENSE |

Circle the best estimate.

4. 78 + 17

about 70   about 80   about 90

© Houghton Mifflin Harcourt Publishing Company

Problem Solving

TOO LITTLE INFORMATION

**Do you have enough information? If you do, solve.
If you do not, circle the sentence you need.
Then solve. Show your work.**

1. In his first turn, Hank moved 12 spaces
   on the game board. On his next turn,
   he moved 11 spaces. How many spaces
   did he move?

   The board has 64 spaces.
   Hank has played the game 8 times.   _____ spaces

2. The game has two kinds of cards.
   It has 25 yellow cards. How many
   cards does the game have all together?

   The game has 35 red cards.
   Hank played the game for 20 minutes.   _____ cards

REASONING

Circle the answer.

3. A spinner has 4 numbers. The pattern of the numbers
   is + 2. What do you need to know to find the numbers?

   the sum of   any one of   the first number
   the numbers   the numbers

© Houghton Mifflin Harcourt Publishing Company

Adding More Than Two Addends

Estimate each addend and the sum.

1.
$$
\begin{array}{r}
23 \quad \underline{20} \\
19 \quad \underline{20} \\
+\ 43 \quad +\underline{40} \\
\hline
\text{about} \quad \underline{80}
\end{array}
\qquad
\begin{array}{r}
36 \quad \underline{\quad} \\
18 \quad \underline{\quad} \\
+\ 31 \quad +\underline{\quad} \\
\hline
\text{about} \quad \underline{\quad}
\end{array}
\qquad
\begin{array}{r}
18 \quad \underline{\quad} \\
22 \quad \underline{\quad} \\
+\ 32 \quad +\underline{\quad} \\
\hline
\text{about} \quad \underline{\quad}
\end{array}
$$

Find the sum.

2.
$$
\begin{array}{r}
17 \\
32 \\
+\ 19 \\
\hline
\end{array}
\quad
\begin{array}{r}
21 \\
9 \\
+\ 32 \\
\hline
\end{array}
\quad
\begin{array}{r}
61 \\
11 \\
+\ 27 \\
\hline
\end{array}
\quad
\begin{array}{r}
53 \\
21 \\
+\ 8 \\
\hline
\end{array}
\quad
\begin{array}{r}
13 \\
41 \\
+\ 29 \\
\hline
\end{array}
\quad
\begin{array}{r}
28 \\
28 \\
+\ 12 \\
\hline
\end{array}
$$

REASONING

Circle the reasonable answer.
Then write the addition sentence.

3. Which group of coins can help you add 25 + 25 + 25?

   3 nickels   3 dimes   3 quarters

   ___ ◯ ___ ◯ ___ = ___

© Houghton Mifflin Harcourt Publishing Company

Name _____   Date _____

Find Sums for Four Addends

Add.

1.
```
  1
  18
  32
  23
+  3
  76
```

2.
```
  45
  31
  29
+ 72
```

3.
```
  24
  62
  70
+ 33
```

4.
```
  83
  32
  61
+ 22
```

5.
```
  37
  15
  31
+ 12
```

6.
```
  21
  13
  96
+ 18
```

PROBLEM SOLVING

Solve. Show how you solved the problem.

7. Kinza jogs 16 minutes on Monday,
   13 minutes on Tuesday, 9 minutes on
   Wednesday, and 20 minutes on Thursday.
   What is the total number of minutes she jogs?

_____ minutes

© Houghton Mifflin Harcourt Publishing Company

Name _____ Date _____

Exploring 2-Digit Subtraction

Complete the table.

	Show.	Take away.	Do you need to trade? Circle Yes or No.	Trade if you need to. Write how many are left.
1.	3 tens 4 ones	5 ones	(Yes) No	__2__ tens __9__ ones
2.	4 tens 2 ones	7 ones	Yes No	_____ tens _____ ones
3.	2 tens 2 ones	9 ones	Yes No	_____ tens _____ ones
4.	3 tens 7 ones	6 ones	Yes No	_____ tens _____ ones
5.	5 tens 1 one	8 ones	Yes No	_____ tens _____ ones
6.	1 ten 9 ones	9 ones	Yes No	_____ tens _____ ones

NUMBER SENSE

7. Circle the better estimate.

$45 - 5 = 40$, so $45 - 8$ is   greater than 40.

                                  less than 40.

65

© Houghton Mifflin Harcourt Publishing Company

Name _____ Date _____

Understanding 2-Digit Subtraction

Subtract. Trade if you need to.

1.

tens	ones
~~3~~ 4	~~14~~ 4
−	8
3	6

tens	ones
3	9
−	8

tens	ones
3	1
−	9

tens	ones
4	6
−	5

2.

tens	ones
3	3
−	4

tens	ones
2	4
−	7

tens	ones
2	5
−	8

tens	ones
4	8
−	9

3.

tens	ones
3	2
−	8

tens	ones
7	4
−	7

tens	ones
6	3
−	4

tens	ones
5	5
−	6

NUMBER SENSE

4. There are 59 windows. The man has washed 9. How many windows are left? _____

_____

_____ windows

5. There are 23 houses. The woman has taken mail to 8. How many houses are left? _____

_____

_____ houses

© Houghton Mifflin Harcourt Publishing Company

Unit 7
Core Skills Math, Grade 2

2-Digit Subtraction

Do you need to trade? Circle <u>Yes</u> or <u>No</u>. Subtract.

1.

tens	ones	
5	8	Yes
−	3	(No)
5	5	

tens	ones	
4	3	Yes
−	2	No

tens	ones	
3	2	Yes
−	9	No

2.

tens	ones	
3	8	Yes
−	9	No

tens	ones	
3	5	Yes
−	7	No

tens	ones	
8	4	Yes
−	9	No

3.

tens	ones	
4	6	Yes
−	7	No

tens	ones	
3	2	Yes
−	6	No

tens	ones	
9	7	Yes
−	6	No

NUMBER SENSE

4. Tamara had 4 dimes and 7 pennies.
She traded one of her dimes for 10 pennies.
Write how many dimes and pennies she
has now.

_____ dimes _____ pennies

© Houghton Mifflin Harcourt Publishing Company

Model Regrouping for Subtraction

Draw to show the regrouping. Write the difference two ways. Write the tens and ones. Write the number.

1. Subtract 9 from 35.

Tens	Ones

____2____ tens ____6____ ones

____26____

2. Subtract 14 from 52.

Tens	Ones

_____ tens _____ ones

_____

3. Subtract 17 from 46.

Tens	Ones

_____ tens _____ ones

_____

4. Subtract 28 from 63.

Tens	Ones

_____ tens _____ ones

_____

PROBLEM SOLVING

Choose a way to solve. Write or draw to explain.

5. Mr. Ortega made 51 cookies.
He gave 14 cookies away. How
many cookies does he have now?   _____ cookies

68

© Houghton Mifflin Harcourt Publishing Company

More 2-Digit Subtraction

Do you need to trade?
Circle Yes or No.
Then subtract.

1.
   5 15
   ~~65~~ (Yes)
   − 39 No
   26

   29 Yes
   − 17 No

   92 Yes
   − 23 No

   44 Yes
   − 21 No

2.
   54 Yes
   − 6 No

   74 Yes
   − 57 No

   99 Yes
   − 27 No

   81 Yes
   − 24 No

3.
   66 Yes
   − 29 No

   95 Yes
   − 16 No

   87 Yes
   − 6 No

   85 Yes
   − 13 No

PROBLEM SOLVING

Solve. Show your work.

4. Glen had 84¢. He paid 25¢ to cross the bridge. How much did he have left?

   _____
   − _____
   _____

   _____ ¢

5. Nicole had 5 dimes and 7 pennies. She used 25¢ to cross the bridge. What coins did she have left?

   _____ dimes

   _____ pennies

   _____
   − _____
   _____

69

Name _____ Date _____

Subtraction Practice

Subtract. Use the code to find a secret message.
Write the code letter in the circle under each answer.

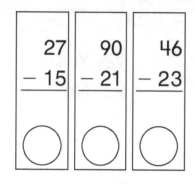

1.
$$\begin{array}{r} 65 \\ -39 \\ \hline 26 \end{array}$$
Ⓘ

$$\begin{array}{r} 27 \\ -15 \\ \hline \end{array}$$ ◯

$$\begin{array}{r} 90 \\ -21 \\ \hline \end{array}$$ ◯

$$\begin{array}{r} 46 \\ -23 \\ \hline \end{array}$$ ◯

$$\begin{array}{r} 54 \\ -6 \\ \hline \end{array}$$ ◯

$$\begin{array}{r} 66 \\ -40 \\ \hline \end{array}$$ ◯

$$\begin{array}{r} 56 \\ -19 \\ \hline \end{array}$$ ◯

$$\begin{array}{r} 94 \\ -15 \\ \hline \end{array}$$ ◯

$$\begin{array}{r} 60 \\ -48 \\ \hline \end{array}$$ ◯

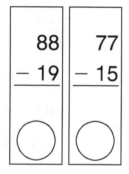

$$\begin{array}{r} 88 \\ -19 \\ \hline \end{array}$$ ◯

$$\begin{array}{r} 77 \\ -15 \\ \hline \end{array}$$ ◯

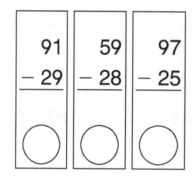

$$\begin{array}{r} 91 \\ -29 \\ \hline \end{array}$$ ◯

$$\begin{array}{r} 59 \\ -28 \\ \hline \end{array}$$ ◯

$$\begin{array}{r} 97 \\ -25 \\ \hline \end{array}$$ ◯

$$\begin{array}{r} 79 \\ -27 \\ \hline \end{array}$$ ◯

$$\begin{array}{r} 42 \\ -5 \\ \hline \end{array}$$ ◯

$$\begin{array}{r} 85 \\ -48 \\ \hline \end{array}$$ ◯

CODE BOX										
12	23	26	31	37	48	52	62	69	72	79
S	W	I	H	O	L	Z	T	A	E	N

NUMBER SENSE

2. Use the code. Make up a secret word.
   Write a subtraction sentence for each letter.
   Have a friend find your word.

70

© Houghton Mifflin Harcourt Publishing Company

Unit 7
Core Skills Math, Grade 2

Name _____   Date _____

Checking Subtraction

Subtract. Then check by adding.

1.
$$67 \quad 55$$
$$-12 \quad +12$$
$$\overline{55} \quad \overline{67}$$

$$87 \quad \underline{}$$
$$-48 \quad \underline{}$$
$$\underline{}$$

$$92 \quad \underline{}$$
$$-57 \quad \underline{}$$
$$\underline{}$$

2.
$$83 \quad \underline{}$$
$$-77 \quad \underline{}$$
$$\underline{}$$

$$45 \quad \underline{}$$
$$-30 \quad \underline{}$$
$$\underline{}$$

$$54 \quad \underline{}$$
$$-21 \quad \underline{}$$
$$\underline{}$$

3.
$$61 \quad \underline{}$$
$$-32 \quad \underline{}$$
$$\underline{}$$

$$80 \quad \underline{}$$
$$-28 \quad \underline{}$$
$$\underline{}$$

$$72 \quad \underline{}$$
$$-55 \quad \underline{}$$
$$\underline{}$$

PROBLEM SOLVING

Solve. Show your work.

4. Suki drew 30 pictures last year. Bobby drew 19 pictures last year. How many more pictures did Suki draw?

_____ more pictures

5. Vince drew 27 pictures last year. He drew 15 pictures this year. How many pictures did he draw all together?

_____ pictures

© Houghton Mifflin Harcourt Publishing Company

Problem Solving

CHOOSE THE OPERATION

Add or subtract to solve.

1. Albert counted 52 animal books.
He put 36 of them on the library
shelves. How many animal books
were left?

_____16_____ animal books

2. Luisa counted 67 fiction books.
Her friend Renée counted 14 more.
How many fiction books did they
count in all?

_____ fiction books

3. Jeff has 37 books. Keith has
13 books. How many more books
does Jeff have than Keith?

_____ more books

REASONING

Circle the best estimate.

4. Georgia used 11 CDs to fill a box.
About how many CDs would she
use to fill 4 boxes?

about 30

about 40

about 50

© Houghton Mifflin Harcourt Publishing Company

Addition and Subtraction Practice

Add or subtract. Find a pattern from
each starting point. Connect the dots
for the two sets of answers.

$$54 \quad 54$$
$$+\ 33 \quad -\ 42$$
$$87 \quad 12$$

Start → • ──── • ← Start

$$54 \qquad 54 \qquad 54$$
$$+\ 34 \qquad -\ 41 \qquad -\ 40$$

•　　　•　　　•

$$54 \qquad 54 \qquad\qquad 54 \qquad 54$$
$$+\ 36 \qquad +\ 35 \qquad\qquad -\ 39 \qquad -\ 38$$

•　　　•　　　　　•　　　•

$$54 \qquad 54 \qquad 54 \qquad\qquad\qquad 54$$
$$+\ 39 \qquad +\ 38 \qquad +\ 37 \qquad\qquad\qquad -\ 37$$

•　　　•　　　•　　　　　　　•

$$54 \quad 54 \quad 54 \quad 54 \quad 54 \quad 54 \quad 54$$
$$+\ 40 \quad +\ 41 \quad +\ 42 \quad -\ 33 \quad -\ 34 \quad -\ 35 \quad -\ 36$$

•　　　•　　•───•　　　•　　　•　　　•

STORY CORNER

Make up a word problem about cars and trucks in a city.
Have a friend solve your problem.

© Houghton Mifflin Harcourt Publishing Company

Name _____ Date _____

Problem Solving

FIND THE REASONABLE ANSWER

Circle the answer that makes sense.

1. Miguel had 6 spaceships.
He lost 2. How many does
he have now?

    8 spaceships
    4 spaceships
    40 spaceships

2. Pete had 44 pennies.
He gave Sue 12. How
many does he have now?

    32 pennies
    56 pennies
    320 pennies

3. Corliss is 5 years old.
Laura is 3 years older.
How old is Laura?

    10 years old
    2 years old
    8 years old

4. There are 26 boys and 12 girls
on the bus. How many children
are there in all?

    38 children
    14 children
    140 children

VISUAL THINKING

5. Look at the graph.
How many trips did
Zeeb make? Circle the
answer that makes sense.

    3 trips

    10 trips

    30 trips

Trips to Earth

		🛸
	🛸	🛸
	🛸	🛸
🛸	🛸	🛸
Jath	Zeeb	Lork

1 🛸 means 10 trips.

© Houghton Mifflin Harcourt Publishing Company

Name _____ Date _____

Problem Solving

| USE DATA |

CESAR'S SPORTING GOODS

| 87 Baseballs | 92 Footballs | 36 Soccer balls |
| 79 Basketballs | 56 Volleyballs | 43 Golf balls |

Use the sign to solve the problems.

1. How many more footballs are there than volleyballs?

$$\begin{array}{r} 92 \\ -\ 56 \\ \hline 36 \end{array}$$

__36__ more footballs

2. How many golf balls and soccer balls are there?

_____

_____ balls

3. How many volleyballs and golf balls are there?

_____

_____ balls

4. How many more basketballs are there than soccer balls?

_____

_____ more basketballs

5. 58 baseballs were sold. How many were not sold?

_____

_____ baseballs

6. 47 basketballs were sold. How many were not sold?

_____

_____ basketballs

75

Solve Multistep Problems

Complete the bar models for the steps you do to solve the problem.

1. Greg has 60 building blocks. His sister gives him 17 more blocks. He uses 38 blocks to make a tower. How many blocks are not used in the tower?

60	17

_77_

38	_____

_77_

_____ blocks

2. Jenna has a train of 26 connecting cubes and a train of 37 connecting cubes. She gives 15 cubes to a friend. How many cubes does Jenna have now?

26	37

_____

15	_____

_____ cubes

_____

PROBLEM SOLVING

Solve. Write or draw to explain.

3. Ava has 25 books. She gives away 7 books. Then Tom gives her 12 books. How many books does Ava have now?

_____ books

© Houghton Mifflin Harcourt Publishing Company

Making Plane Figures

1. Color the circles blue. Color the triangles orange.
Color the rectangles red.

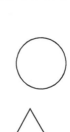
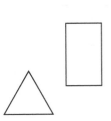

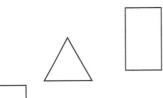

2. Count each shape. Write how many.

_____ circles   _____ triangles   _____ rectangles

3. Color the squares green. Color the triangles purple.
Color the circles red.

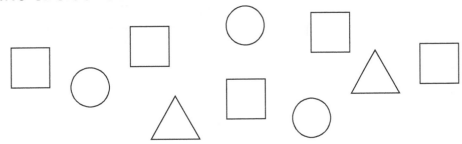

4. How many are there? Count each shape. Write how many.

_____ squares   _____ triangles   _____ circles

VISUAL THINKING

5. If you traced around the widest part of a cone,
what plane figure would you draw?

rectangle   circle   triangle

© Houghton Mifflin Harcourt Publishing Company

Sides and Corners

1. Draw a shape that has 8 sides and 8 corners.

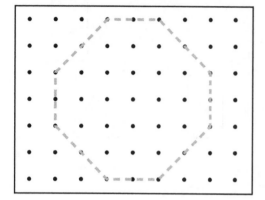

2. Draw a shape that has 5 sides and 5 corners.

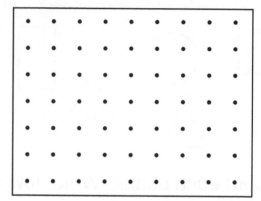

3. Draw a shape that has 3 sides and 3 corners.

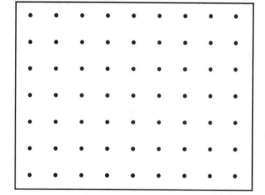

4. Draw a shape that has 4 sides and 4 corners. Make all 4 sides the same length.

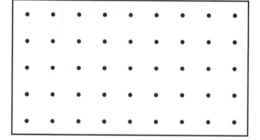

VISUAL THINKING

5. In this box, draw a shape that has sides and corners. Cover it.

Describe it to a friend. Have your friend draw it. Compare your shape with the one your friend drew.

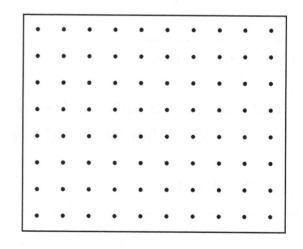

78

© Houghton Mifflin Harcourt Publishing Company

Exploring Plane Figures and Polygons

A polygon is a closed figure. It has straight sides.
Circle the polygons.

1.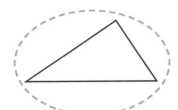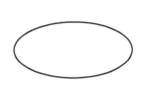

2.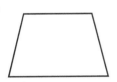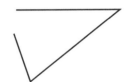

3.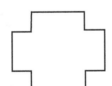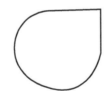

REASONING

Circle the answer.

4. If an octopus has 8 legs, what figure has 8 sides?

    oval   pentagon   octagon

5. If a tricycle has 3 wheels, what figure has 3 sides?

    bicycle   triangle   rectangle

© Houghton Mifflin Harcourt Publishing Company

Unit 8
Core Skills Math, Grade 2

Name _____ Date _____

Congruent Figures

Look at each figure. Use a geoboard to make a figure that is the same size and shape. Draw your figure.

1.

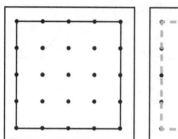

2.

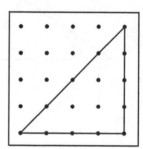

3.

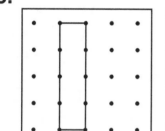

4.

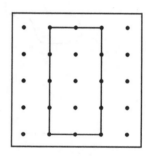
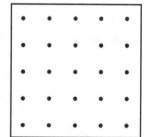

5.

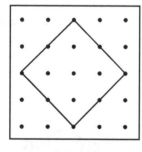
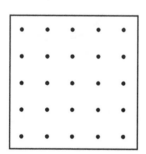

6.

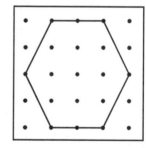
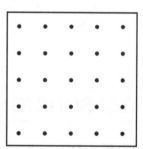

REASONING

7. Use a pattern block. Copy this design.

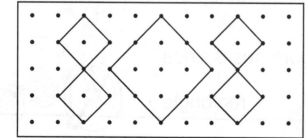

80

© Houghton Mifflin Harcourt Publishing Company

Name _____ Date _____

Polygons

A regular polygon has equal sides.
All corners are the same size. Circle the regular polygons.

1.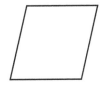

2.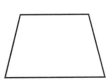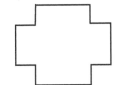

3.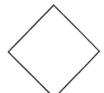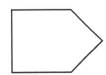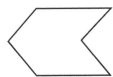

VISUAL THINKING

4. Circle two ways to name a square.

closed figure   polygon   open figure

5. Are all squares regular? Circle **Yes** or **No**.

Yes   No

6. Are all rectangles regular? Circle **Yes** or **No**.

Yes   No

81

Partition Rectangles

How many 1-inch punch-out squares will fit in each space?
First, write your guess. Then use 1-inch squares to check.

1.

Guess. _____ squares   Check. __10__ squares

2.

Guess. _____ squares   Check. _____ squares

3.

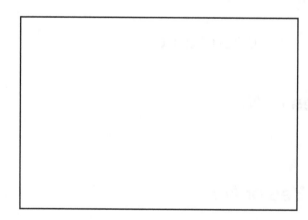

Guess. _____ squares

Check. _____ squares

© Houghton Mifflin Harcourt Publishing Company

Partition Rectangles and Squares

Use 1-inch punch-out squares to cover the rectangle.
Trace around the squares. Write how many.

1.

Number of rows: _2_

Number of columns: _3_

Total: _6_ square tiles

2.

Number of rows: _____

Number of columns: _____

Total: _____ square tiles

PROBLEM SOLVING

Solve. Write or draw to explain.

3. Nina wants to put color tiles on a square. 3 color tiles fit across the top of the square. How many rows and columns of squares will Nina need? How many color tiles will she use in all?

_____ tiles

Number of rows: _____

Number of columns: _____

Total: _____ square tiles

© Houghton Mifflin Harcourt Publishing Company

Name _____ Date _____

Equal Parts

Write the number of equal parts.

1.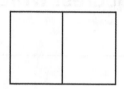

___8___ _____ _____ _____

2.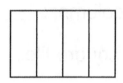

_____ _____ _____ _____

3.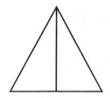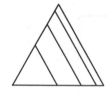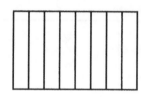

_____ _____ _____ _____

4.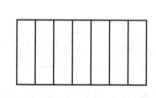

_____ _____ _____ _____

| **PROBLEM SOLVING** |

5. Four friends want to share
two apples in equal parts.
Show how they can divide them.

© Houghton Mifflin Harcourt Publishing Company

Name _____ Date _____

Equal Shares

Draw to show your answer.

1. Max has square pizzas that are the same size.
   What are two different ways he can divide the
   pizzas into fourths?

2. Lia has two pieces of paper that are the same size.
   What are two different ways she can divide the
   pieces of paper into halves?

3. Frank has two crackers that are the same size.
   What are two different ways he can divide the
   crackers into thirds?

© Houghton Mifflin Harcourt Publishing Company

Name _____ Date _____

Fractions

1. Color $\frac{1}{3}$.

   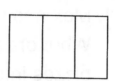

2. Color $\frac{1}{4}$.

3. Color $\frac{1}{8}$.

   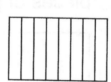

REASONING

Circle <u>Yes</u> or <u>No</u>.

4. Henry colored $\frac{1}{2}$ of a circle.

Marsha colored $\frac{1}{2}$ of a larger circle.

Did they color the same amount?

Yes   No

© Houghton Mifflin Harcourt Publishing Company

Name _____ Date _____

More Fractions

Complete each fraction to show what part is shaded.

1. 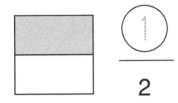 $\dfrac{1}{2}$ $\dfrac{}{3}$ $\dfrac{}{4}$

2. 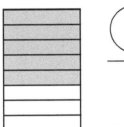 $\dfrac{}{8}$  $\dfrac{}{8}$ 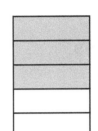 $\dfrac{}{5}$

Write a fraction to show what part is shaded.

3. 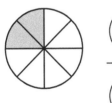 $\dfrac{2}{8}$ 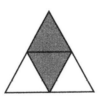 $\dfrac{}{}$ 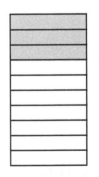 $\dfrac{}{}$

4. 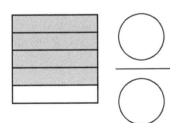 $\dfrac{}{}$ 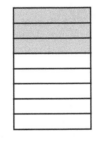 $\dfrac{}{}$ 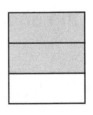 $\dfrac{}{}$

VISUAL THINKING

5. Circle the fractions that are the same size.

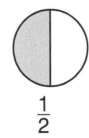

$\dfrac{1}{2}$ $\dfrac{1}{3}$ $\dfrac{2}{4}$

© Houghton Mifflin Harcourt Publishing Company

Inches and Feet

Use an inch ruler to draw pieces of yarn.

1. 2 inches

2. 5 inches

3. 3 inches

Color blue the longest piece of yarn.
Color red the shortest piece of yarn.

NUMBER SENSE

Think about the real object. Circle the better estimate.

4.

shorter than 1 foot
longer than 1 foot

5.

shorter than 1 foot
longer than 1 foot

© Houghton Mifflin Harcourt Publishing Company

Problem Solving

ESTIMATE AND MEASURE

Circle the reasonable answer. Then use an inch ruler to measure the length to the nearest inch. Write the length.

		Estimate	Measure
1.	an eraser	1 inch (7 inches) 20 inches	about _____ inches
2.	your thumb	2 inches 9 inches 15 inches	about _____ inches
3.	a calculator	25 inches 15 inches 5 inches	about _____ inches

NUMBER SENSE

Write an estimate.

4.

about _____ long

© Houghton Mifflin Harcourt Publishing Company

Name _____ Date _____

Exploring Length: Inch

Measure the length of each in inches.

1.

_____

2.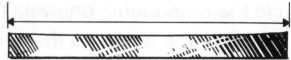

_____

3.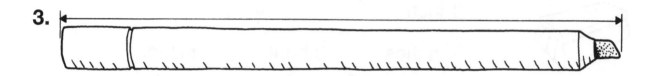

_____

Draw each length from the •.

4. 2 inches •

5. 1 inch •

6. 4 inches •

7. Find two things in your home that measure about 9 inches each.

_____

REASONING

8. Yoshi glues his report to a piece of art paper. The report paper is 8 inches wide. It is 10 inches long. The art paper makes a 1-inch border all around. How wide is the art paper?

_____

90

Name _____ Date _____

Choose a Tool

Choose the best tool for measuring the real object. Then measure and record the length or distance.

inch ruler
yardstick
measuring tape

1. the length of your desk

Tool: _____

Length: _____

2. the distance around a basket

Tool: _____

Length: _____

PROBLEM SOLVING

Choose the better tool for measuring. Explain your choice.

3. Mark wants to measure the length of his room. Should he use an inch ruler or a yardstick?

Mark should use _____ because

_____

_____

© Houghton Mifflin Harcourt Publishing Company

Measure in Inches and Feet

Measure to the nearest inch.
Then measure to the nearest foot.

Find the real object.	Measure.
1. bookcase	_____ inches _____ feet
2. window	_____ inches _____ feet
3. chair	_____ inches _____ feet

PROBLEM SOLVING

4. Jake has a piece of yarn that is 4 feet long.
Blair has a piece of yarn that is 4 inches long.
Who has the longer piece of yarn? Explain.

_____

_____

92

Length: Foot, Yard, Mile

Circle the better estimate.

1. length of a piece of paper

(1 foot)   1 yard

2. length of a football field

100 yards   100 miles

3. length of a classroom

10 yards   10 miles

4. distance from home to school

2 yards   2 miles

5. height of a chair

2 feet   2 yards

6. distance a car travels

20 yards   20 miles

REASONING

Solve. Draw a picture or explain.

7. Jeremiah plants tomato plants.
He spaces them 18 inches apart.
How many inches is the third
plant from the first plant?

_____ inches

8. Jeremiah planted lettuce in rows.
The rows are 12 inches apart.
How many inches is the fourth
row from the first row?

_____ inches

© Houghton Mifflin Harcourt Publishing Company

Name _____ Date _____

Centimeters

Use your centimeter ruler to draw pieces of yarn.

1. 7 centimeters

2. 3 centimeters

3. 11 centimeters

**This string is 10 centimeters long.
It is 1 decimeter long. Work with a friend.**

4. Measure and cut a string that is
as long as a decimeter. Use your
string to find something that is
longer. Write the name of the
object you found. _____

NUMBER SENSE

5. Hal's card is 3 centimeters wider than
Meg's. Meg's card is 7 centimeters wide.
How wide is Hal's card?   _____ centimeters

94

Name _____ Date _____

More Measurement

Make a ruler. Cut a strip of paper 10 centimeters long.

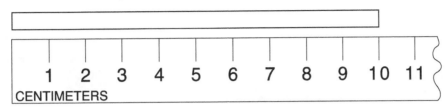

Draw an X to show your estimate. Then use your ruler to check.

Draw a ✓ to show your measurement.

Objects	More than 10 centimeters	Less than 10 centimeters	About 10 centimeters
1. your arm	X ✓		
2. your shoe			
3. clock			
4. eraser			

REASONING

5. 1 decimeter = 10 centimeters,

so 2 decimeters = _____ centimeters.

© Houghton Mifflin Harcourt Publishing Company

Exploring Length: Centimeter

Measure the length of each in centimeters.

1.

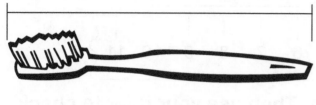

_____ centimeters

2.

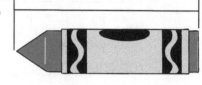

_____ centimeters

Draw each length from the •.

3. 2 centimeters •

4. 3 centimeters •

5. 12 centimeters •

REASONING

A new crayon is about 8 centimeters long.
Use a crayon to estimate length.

6. length of your pencil

   _____ crayons

   _____ centimeters

7. length of your hand

   _____ crayons

   _____ centimeters

© Houghton Mifflin Harcourt Publishing Company

Name _____ Date _____

Measure and Compare Lengths

Measure the length of each object. Write a number sentence to find the difference between the lengths.

1.

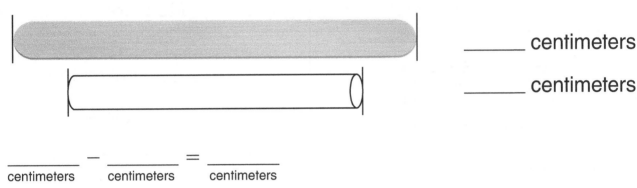

_____ centimeters

_____ centimeters

_____ − _____ = _____
centimeters   centimeters   centimeters

The craft stick is _____ centimeters longer than the chalk.

2.

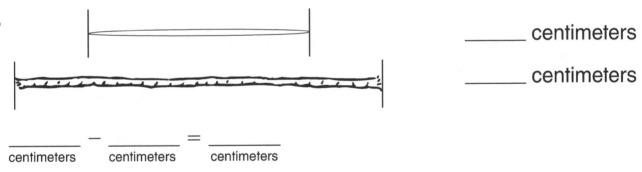

_____ centimeters

_____ centimeters

_____ − _____ = _____
centimeters   centimeters   centimeters

The string is _____ centimeters longer than the toothpick.

PROBLEM SOLVING

Solve. Write or draw to explain.

3. A string is 11 centimeters long, a ribbon is 24 centimeters long, and a large paper clip is 5 centimeters long. How much longer is the ribbon than the string?

_____ centimeters

© Houghton Mifflin Harcourt Publishing Company

Centimeters and Meters

Measure to the nearest centimeter.
Then measure to the nearest meter.

Find the real object.	Measure.
1. bookcase	_____ centimeters _____ meters
2. window	_____ centimeters _____ meters
3. map	_____ centimeters _____ meters

PROBLEM SOLVING

4. Sally will measure the length of a wall in
both centimeters and meters. Will there
be fewer centimeters or fewer meters? Explain.

_____

_____

_____

© Houghton Mifflin Harcourt Publishing Company

Name _____ Date _____

Exploring Length: Meter and Kilometer

Circle the better estimate.

1. length of a chalkboard

　　3 meters　　　30 meters

2. height of a child

　　1 meter　　　5 meters

3. height of your desk

　　more than 1 meter

　　less than 1 meter

4. height of a door

　　more than 1 meter

　　less than 1 meter

5. distance an airplane flies

　　more than 1 kilometer

　　less than 1 kilometer

6. distance from your classroom
to the school office

　　more than 1 kilometer

　　less than 1 kilometer

PROBLEM SOLVING

Solve.

7. Jared can run 1 kilometer in about
8 minutes. How long will it take him to
run 3 kilometers at the same speed?

_____ minutes

8. In the softball toss, Abby threw distances
of 28 meters and 37 meters. What is the
distance altogether?

_____ meters

© Houghton Mifflin Harcourt Publishing Company

Name _____ Date _____

Exploring Units of Measure

Find the length of each object to the nearest centimeter and inch.

	Object	Centimeters	Inches
1.	a marker		
2.	a crayon		
3.	a paper clip		
4.	a folder		
5.	a pencil		

Solve.

6. Max measures his math book in inches and centimeters. Which measurement has fewer units?

_____

– – – – – – – – – – – – – – – –

_____

VISUAL THINKING

Use the pictures to solve.

7. Suzi and Amy measure the length of a hallway. They count their steps. Which girl counts more steps?

Suzi   Amy

© Houghton Mifflin Harcourt Publishing Company

Name _____ Date _____

Add and Subtract in Inches

Draw a diagram. Write a number sentence using a ▮ for the missing number. Solve.

1. Molly had a ribbon that was 23 inches long. She cut 7 inches off the ribbon. How long is her ribbon now?

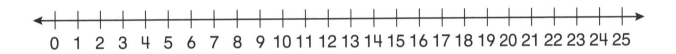

_____

Molly's ribbon is _____ inches long now.

2. Jed has a paper clip chain that is 11 inches long. He adds 7 inches of paper clips to the chain. How long is the paper clip chain now?

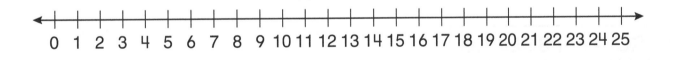

_____

The paper clip chain is _____ inches long now.

© Houghton Mifflin Harcourt Publishing Company

Name _____ Date _____

Display Measurement Data

1. Use an inch ruler.
   Measure and record the
   lengths of 4 different books
   in inches.

1st book: _____ inches	
2nd book: _____ inches	
3rd book: _____ inches	
4th book: _____ inches	

2. Make a line plot of the information above.
   Write a title for the line plot. Then write the
   numbers and draw the **X**s.

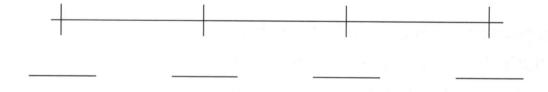

PROBLEM SOLVING

3. Jesse measured the lengths of some strings.
   Use his list to complete the line plot.

Lengths of Strings
5 inches
7 inches
6 inches
8 inches
5 inches

© Houghton Mifflin Harcourt Publishing Company

Name _____ Date _____

Collect Data

1. Take a survey. Ask 10 classmates how they got to school. Use tally marks to show their choices.

How We Got to School	
Way	**Tally**
walk	
bus	
car	
bike	

2. How many classmates rode in a bus to school?

_____ classmates

3. How many classmates rode in a car to school?

_____ classmates

4. In which way did the fewest classmates get to school?

_____

5. In which way did the most classmates get to school?

_____

6. Did more classmates get to school by walking or by riding in a car?

How many more?   _____ more classmates

© Houghton Mifflin Harcourt Publishing Company

Problem Solving

USE DATA

Some children voted for their favorite things to do in the summer.
Count the tally marks. Write the totals in the table.

Summer Activities		
	Tally Marks	Total
	~~IIII~~ ~~IIII~~ ~~IIII~~ ~~IIII~~ ~~IIII~~ I	26
	~~IIII~~ ~~IIII~~ ~~IIII~~ II	
	~~IIII~~ III	
	~~IIII~~ ~~IIII~~ III	

Answer the questions about the table.

1. How many children like
to go camping in
the summer?

_____ children

2. What is the total number of
children who like to skate
and play baseball?

_____ children

3. Which summer activity did
the greatest number of
children vote for?

STORY CORNER

4. Make up a question about
the table. Give it to a friend
to answer.

_____

104

Problem Solving

MAKE A TABLE

1. Some children made this funny bird. How many of
   each shape did they use? Complete the table to find out.

Our Funny Bird	
Shape	Number
◯	2
▢	
▭	
△	

2. How many rectangles would there be in
   4 funny birds like this one? Make a table to find out.

birds	1	2	3	4
rectangles	5	_____	_____	_____

PROBLEM SOLVING

Use the table to answer the questions.

3. How many rectangles
   would there be in
   4 funny birds? _____

4. How many rectangles
   would there be in
   3 funny birds? _____

© Houghton Mifflin Harcourt Publishing Company

Name _____ Date _____

Read Bar Graphs

Use the bar graph.

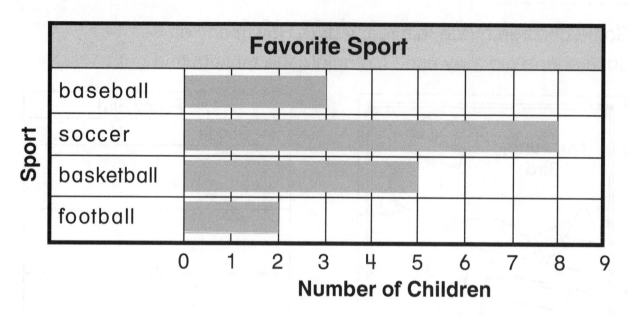

1. How many children chose basketball?   _____5_____ children

2. Which sport did the most children choose? _____

3. How many more children chose basketball
   than baseball?   _____ more children

4. Which sport did the fewest children choose? _____

5. How many children chose a sport that was not soccer?

                                                        _____ children

PROBLEM SOLVING

6. How many children chose
   baseball or basketball?   _____ children

© Houghton Mifflin Harcourt Publishing Company

Name _____ Date _____

Problem Solving

MAKE A BAR GRAPH

What is the favorite forest animal of your friends?
Ask each child to choose his or her favorite animal.
Write a tally mark | to show each answer. Find the total
for each animal. Then complete your graph.

1.

Animal	Tally Marks	Total
Rabbit		
Squirrel		
Deer		
Raccoon		

2.

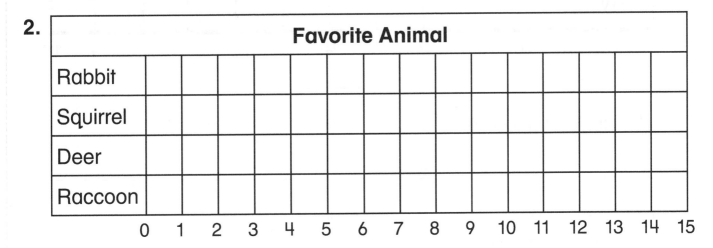

VISUAL THINKING

Circle your answer.

3. Which bar on your graph shows you the least favorite animal?

longest bar   shortest bar

© Houghton Mifflin Harcourt Publishing Company

Name _____ Date _____

Display Data

Make a bar graph to solve the problem.

1. The list shows the number of books that Abby read each month. Describe how the number of books she read changed from February to May.

February	8 books
March	7 books
April	6 books
May	4 books

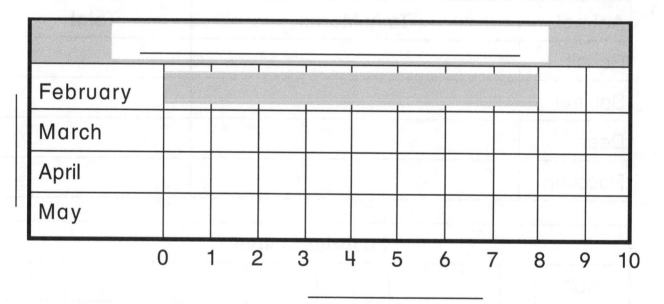

The number of books _____

_____

2. How many books in all did Abby read in February and March?

_____ books

3. How many fewer books did Abby read in April than in February?

_____ fewer books

4. In which months did Abby read fewer than 7 books? _____

_____

© Houghton Mifflin Harcourt Publishing Company

Name _____   Date _____

Problem Solving

Children Who Went to the Circus

Group A	♀ ♀ ♀ ♀ ♀
Group B	♀ ♀ ♀ ♀
Group C	♀ ♀
Group D	♀ ♀ ♀

Each ♀ stands for 4 children.

Read the graph. Then answer each question.

1. How many children are in Group D?

_____ children

2. How many children are in Group B?

_____ children

3. Which group had the fewest children?

Group _____

4. What is the total number of children in Groups A and C?

_____ children

REASONING

Suppose each ♀ meant 2 children. Circle the answers.

5. Would your answer to question 3 change?

Yes   No

6. What would your answer to question 2 be now?

8 children   32 children

© Houghton Mifflin Harcourt Publishing Company

Name _____   Date _____

Read Picture Graphs

Use the picture graph to answer the questions.

Number of Books Read						
Ryan	📖	📖	📖	📖		
Gwen	📖	📖				
Anna	📖	📖	📖	📖	📖	📖
Henry	📖	📖	📖			

Key: Each 📖 stands for 1 book.

1. How many books in all did Henry and
   Anna read?   ___9___ books

2. How many more books did Ryan read
   than Gwen?   _____ more books

3. How many fewer books did Gwen read
   than Anna?   _____ fewer books

4. How many books did the four children
   read in all?   _____ books

PROBLEM SOLVING

Use the picture graph above. Write or draw to explain.

5. Carlos read 4 books. How many children
   read fewer books than Carlos?   _____ children

© Houghton Mifflin Harcourt Publishing Company

Name _____ Date _____

Problem Solving

MAKE A PICTOGRAPH

Read the pictograph. Then answer each question.

Number of Circus Tickets Sold	
Wednesday	🎫 🎫 🎫
Thursday	🎫 🎫
Friday	🎫 🎫 🎫 🎫
Saturday	🎫 🎫 🎫 🎫 🎫 🎫

Each 🎫 stands for 10 tickets.

1. On which day were the fewest tickets sold? _____

2. How many more tickets were sold on
Friday than on Thursday? _____

**Make a pictograph of lunch choices. Use 😊 to show children.
Have 1 😊 stand for 2 children.**

3. There are 12 children who
bring lunch. There are 4
children who buy hot lunch
and 8 children who buy
cold lunch.

Bring	
Buy hot	
Buy cold	

Each 😊 stands for 2 children.

4. Write a title at the top of your graph.

NUMBER SENSE

5. Suppose you made a pictograph to show lunch choices for 25, 15,
and 10 children. How many children would you have each symbol
stand for? Explain. _____

_____

© Houghton Mifflin Harcourt Publishing Company

Name _____ Date _____

Exploring Hundreds

Use hundreds to show each number. Write the number.

1. 2 hundred _200_

2. 4 hundred _400_

3. 6 hundred _600_

4. 8 hundred _800_

5. 9 hundred _900_

6. 7 hundred _700_

7. 5 hundred _500_

8. 3 hundred _300_

9. 1 hundred _100_

NUMBER SENSE

Write the numbers.

10. _390_

11. _400_

112

© Houghton Mifflin Harcourt Publishing Company

Group Tens as Hundreds

Write how many tens. Circle groups of 10 tens.
Write how many hundreds. Write the number.

1.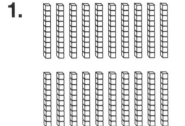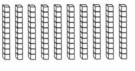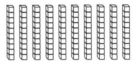

_40_ tens

_4_ hundreds

_400_

2.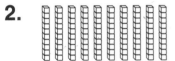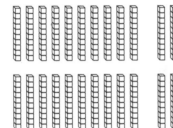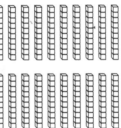

_60_ tens

_6_ hundreds

_____

3.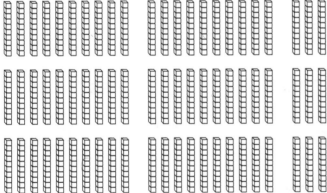

_90_ tens

_9_ hundreds

_____

PROBLEM SOLVING

Solve. Write or draw to explain.

4. Farmer Gray has 30 flowerpots.
He planted 10 seeds in each pot.
How many seeds did he plant?

_300_ seeds

© Houghton Mifflin Harcourt Publishing Company

Name _____ Date _____

Exploring 3-Digit Numbers

Count. Write the number.

1.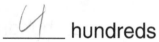

   ___3___ hundreds ___2___ tens ___4___ ones ___324___

2.

   ___5___ hundreds ___6___ tens ___1___ ones ___561___

3.

   ___4___ hundreds ___3___ tens ___5___ ones ___435___

REASONING

Circle the most reasonable answer.

4. Cliff is ___8___ years older
   than his brother.

   (8)   80   800

5. There are ___40___ children on
   the full school bus.

   4   (40)   400

6. There are ___200___ seats in
   the movie theater.

   2   20   (200)

7. The movie is ___3___
   hours long.

   (3)   30   300

© Houghton Mifflin Harcourt Publishing Company

Understanding Hundreds, Tens, and Ones

Work with a friend. Use place-value models.

1. Show the number. Add 10 more. Continue adding 10 more. Complete the table.

	hundreds	tens	ones
640	6	4	0
650	6	5	0

2. Show the number. Add 100 more. Continue adding 100 more. Complete the table.

	hundreds	tens	ones
300	3	0	0

NUMBER SENSE

Circle the models that show the same number.
Use place-value models if you need to.

3.

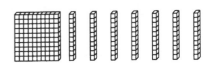

© Houghton Mifflin Harcourt Publishing Company

Name _____ Date _____

Writing Numbers to 999

Look at the models. Write how many in the chart.
Then write the number.

1.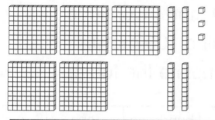

hundreds	tens	ones
5	4	3

543

2.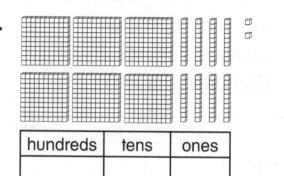

hundreds	tens	ones

_____

3.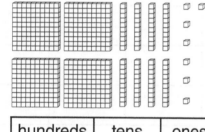

hundreds	tens	ones

_____

4.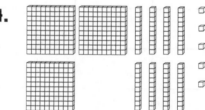

hundreds	tens	ones

_____

5.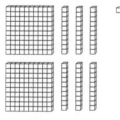

hundreds	tens	ones

_____

6.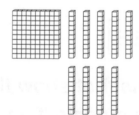

hundreds	tens	ones

_____

NUMBER SENSE

7. Write the number that is
   10 greater than 173. _____

8. Write the number that is
   100 greater than 731. _____

116

Place Value

Read the number in the chart. Write how many.

1.

hundreds	tens	ones
7	2	8

___7___ hundreds   _700_

___2___ tens   _20_

___8___ ones   _8_

hundreds	tens	ones
2	7	8

_____ hundreds   _____

_____ tens   _____

_____ ones   _____

2.

hundreds	tens	ones
5	1	6

_____ hundreds   _____

_____ tens   _____

_____ ones   _____

hundreds	tens	ones
6	5	1

_____ hundreds   _____

_____ tens   _____

_____ ones   _____

3.

hundreds	tens	ones
4	3	7

_____ hundreds   _____

_____ tens   _____

_____ ones   _____

hundreds	tens	ones
3	4	7

_____ hundreds   _____

_____ tens   _____

_____ ones   _____

NUMBER SENSE

4. Lucas has 7 ones and 9 hundreds. What number does he have? _____

5. Vicki has 2 tens and 6 hundreds. What number does she have? _____

117

More Place Value

Write the number.

1. 4 hundreds 8 tens
7 ones   _487_

2. 500 + 50 + 2 _____

3. 800 + 7   _____

4. 6 hundreds 1 ten 1 one _____

Work with a friend.

5. Fill in the puzzle.

Across

1. 199 + 1
2. 400 + 50
4. 3, 6, _____, 12
5. 7 hundreds 1 ten 8 ones
6. 400 + 50 + 6
9. 700 + 80 + 9
11. 5 hundreds 7 tens 3 ones
13. 200 + 300
14. 4, 8, 12, _____
15. 1 more than 997

Down

1. 2 hundreds 9 tens 4 ones
2. 4 hundreds 1 ten 7 ones
3. 500 + 80 + 8
7. 500 + 50 + 5

8. 6 hundreds 7 tens
10. 900 + 6
12. 1 more than 308
14. 9, _____, 27, 36

NUMBER SENSE

6. Write the number that is
3 hundreds less than 640.   _____

© Houghton Mifflin Harcourt Publishing Company

Number Names

Write the number.

1. two hundred thirty-two

232

2. five hundred forty-four

_____

3. one hundred fifty-eight

_____

4. nine hundred fifty

_____

5. four hundred twenty

_____

6. six hundred seventy-eight

_____

Write the number using words.

7. 317

_____

8. 457

_____

PROBLEM SOLVING

Circle the answer.

9. Six hundred twenty-six children attend
Elm Street School. Which is another
way to write this number?

266   626   662

© Houghton Mifflin Harcourt Publishing Company

Name _____ Date _____

Different Forms of Numbers

Read the number and draw a quick picture.
Then write the number in different ways.

1. two hundred fifty-one   __2__ hundreds __5__ tens __1__ one

    __200__ + __50__ + __1__

    __251__

2. three hundred twelve   _____ hundreds _____ ten _____ ones

    _____ + _____ + _____

    _____

3. two hundred seven   _____ hundreds _____ tens _____ ones

    _____ + _____ + _____

    _____

PROBLEM SOLVING

Write the number another way.

4. 200 + 30 + 7   _____

5. 895   _____

© Houghton Mifflin Harcourt Publishing Company

Compare Numbers Using Models

Write each number. Compare.
Then circle the number that is less.

1.

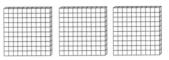

314

_____

2.

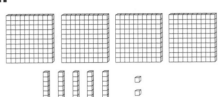

_____

_____

3.

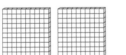

_____

_____

4.

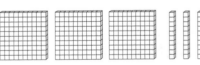

_____

_____

NUMBER SENSE

Use place-value models to compare.
Then circle the number that is less.

5.	167	578	823	424	169
	176	478	923	323	109

© Houghton Mifflin Harcourt Publishing Company

Compare Numbers Using Symbols

Write < or > in the ◯.

1. 139 ⊘ 193   390 ◯ 391   421 ◯ 422

2. 598 ◯ 498   401 ◯ 441   509 ◯ 501

3. 777 ◯ 771   902 ◯ 992   120 ◯ 102

4. 99 ◯ 100   999 ◯ 99   287 ◯ 267

5. 302 ◯ 320   675 ◯ 576   110 ◯ 101

NUMBER SENSE

**Write the numbers in order from least to greatest.
Use place-value models if you need to.**

6. 13, 621, 27, 98, 109, 56, 129

13, _____, _____, _____, _____, _____, 621

7. 82, 208, 802, 28, 280, 820

28, _____, _____, _____, _____, _____

© Houghton Mifflin Harcourt Publishing Company

Compare Numbers

**Model the numbers. Draw quick pictures
to show how you solved the problem.**

1. Lauryn has 128 marbles. Kristin has
118 marbles. Who has more marbles?

_____

2. Nick has 189 trading cards. Kyle has
198 trading cards. Who has fewer cards?

_____

3. A piano has 36 black keys and
52 white keys. Are there more black
keys or white keys on a piano?

_____

4. There are 253 pecans in a bag. There
are 266 pecans in a box. Are there
fewer pecans in the bag or in the box?

_____

© Houghton Mifflin Harcourt Publishing Company

Numbers to Hundreds

Write the number.

1. $700 + 20 + 3 =$ _723_

2. $100 + 0 + 9 =$ _____

3. $400 + 70 + 5 =$ _____

4. $300 + 10 + 6 =$ _____

5. five hundred seventy-nine _____

6. seven hundred forty _____

7. 4 hundreds 8 tens 5 ones _____

8. 6 hundreds 1 ten 0 ones _____

Complete the table. Write the number that is 100 less.
Write the number that is 100 more.

9.

100 Less	Number	100 More
_____	134	_____
_____	456	_____
_____	872	_____
_____	507	_____

REASONING

Circle the most reasonable answer.

10. Julie is in second grade. She is about _____ feet tall.

4   40   400

11. There are about _____ children in Julie's second-grade class.

3   30   300

© Houghton Mifflin Harcourt Publishing Company

Counting Patterns Within 100

Count by ones.

1. 58, 59, __60__, __61__, __62__, __63__, __64__

Count by fives.

2. 45, 50, _____, _____, _____, _____, _____

3. 20, 25, _____, _____, _____, _____, _____

Count by tens.

4. 20, _____, _____, _____, _____, _____, _____

Count back by ones.

5. 87, 86, 85, _____, _____, _____

PROBLEM SOLVING

6. Tim counts his friends' fingers by fives.
He counts six hands. What numbers does he say?

5, _____, _____, _____, _____, _____

© Houghton Mifflin Harcourt Publishing Company

Name _____ Date _____

Counting Patterns Within 1,000

Count by fives.

1. 415, 420, 425, 430, 435, 440

2. 675, 680, _____, _____, _____, _____, _____

Count by tens.

3. 210, 220, _____, _____, _____, _____, _____

4. 840, 850, _____, _____, _____, _____, _____

Count by hundreds.

5. 300, 400, _____, _____, _____, _____, _____

Count back by ones.

6. 953, 952, _____, _____, _____, _____, _____

PROBLEM SOLVING

7. Lee has a jar of 100 pennies.
   She adds groups of 10 pennies to the jar.
   She adds 5 groups. What numbers does she say?

   _____, _____, _____, _____, _____

© Houghton Mifflin Harcourt Publishing Company

Count On and Count Back by 10 and 100

Write the number.

1. 10 more than 451

461

2. 10 less than 770

_____

3. 100 more than 367

_____

4. 100 less than 895

_____

5. 10 less than 812

_____

6. 100 more than 543

_____

7. 10 more than 218

_____

8. 100 more than 379

_____

9. 100 less than 324

_____

10. 10 less than 829

_____

PROBLEM SOLVING

Solve. Write or draw to explain.

11. Sarah has 128 stickers. Alex has 10 fewer stickers than Sarah. How many stickers does Alex have?

_____ stickers

© Houghton Mifflin Harcourt Publishing Company

Number Patterns

Look at the digits to find the next two numbers.

1. 232, 242, 252, 262, ☐ , ☐

The next two numbers are _272_ and _282_.

2. 185, 285, 385, 485, ☐ , ☐

The next two numbers are _____ and _____.

3. 428, 528, 628, 728, ☐ , ☐

The next two numbers are _____ and _____.

4. 654, 664, 674, 684, ☐ , ☐

The next two numbers are _____ and _____.

5. 333, 433, 533, 633, ☐ , ☐

The next two numbers are _____ and _____.

PROBLEM SOLVING

6. What are the missing numbers in the pattern?

431, 441, 451, 461, ☐ , 481, 491, ☐

The missing numbers are _____ and _____.

128

Name _____ Date _____

Names for Numbers

Write the number. Use place-value models if you need to.

1. 60 = __6__ tens

2. 400 = _____ ones

3. 900 = _____ hundreds

4. 800 = _____ tens

5. 70 = _____ ones

6. 320 = _____ tens

Write the value of each number in two ways.

7. 450 = _____ hundreds _____ tens _____ ones

450 = _____ + _____ + _____

8. 503 = _____ hundreds _____ tens _____ ones

503 = _____ + _____ + _____

9. 681 = _____ hundreds _____ tens _____ one

681 = _____ + _____ + _____

NUMBER SENSE

Complete the number patterns.

10. 200, 300, 400, _____, _____, _____, 800

11. 770, 780, 790, _____, _____, _____, 830

12. 362, 372, 382, _____, _____, _____, 422

© Houghton Mifflin Harcourt Publishing Company

Name _____ Date _____

Draw to Represent 3-Digit Addition

Draw quick pictures. Write how many hundreds, tens, and ones in all. Write the number.

1. Add 142 and 215.

Hundreds	Tens	Ones

_____ hundreds _____ tens _____ ones

_____

2. Add 263 and 206.

Hundreds	Tens	Ones

_____ hundreds _____ tens _____ ones

_____

PROBLEM SOLVING

Solve. Write or draw to explain.

3. A farmer sold 324 lemons and 255 limes. How many pieces of fruit did the farmer sell altogether?

_____ pieces of fruit

© Houghton Mifflin Harcourt Publishing Company

Break Apart 3-Digit Addends

Break apart the addends to find the sum.

1. 518 ⟶ 500 + 10 + 8

    + 221 ⟶ _____ + _____ + _____

    _____ + _____ + _____ = _____

2. 438 ⟶ _____ + _____ + _____

    + 142 ⟶ _____ + _____ + _____

    _____ + _____ + _____ = _____

3. 324 ⟶ _____ + _____ + _____

    + 239 ⟶ _____ + _____ + _____

    _____ + _____ + _____ = _____

PROBLEM SOLVING

Solve. Write or draw to explain.

4. There are 126 crayons in a bucket.
   A teacher puts 144 more crayons
   in the bucket. How many crayons
   are in the bucket now?

   _____ crayons

© Houghton Mifflin Harcourt Publishing Company

Name _____ Date _____

Exploring 3-Digit Addition

Use place-value models. Find the sums. Trade if you need to.

1.

hundreds	tens	ones
	1	
3	6	8
+ 1	1	3
4	8	1

hundreds	tens	ones
	☐	
1	8	7
+ 2	1	2

hundreds	tens	ones
	☐	
7	3	4
+	3	6

2.

hundreds	tens	ones
	☐	
4	1	3
+ 3	1	9

hundreds	tens	ones
	☐	
5	5	5
+	4	3

hundreds	tens	ones
	☐	
6	2	7
+ 2	4	6

NUMBER SENSE

Circle your estimate.

Remember
< means less than
> means greater than

3.   400
       + 300
       _____

The sum is < 500.

The sum is > 500.

4.   100
       + 700
       _____

The sum is < 900.

The sum is > 900.

© Houghton Mifflin Harcourt Publishing Company

Understanding 3-Digit Addition

Use place-value models. Add.

1.

hundreds	tens	ones
2	3	7
+ 5	0	2
7	3	9

hundreds	tens	ones
4	2	9
+ 1	1	6

hundreds	tens	ones
3	3	8
+ 2	2	6

2.

hundreds	tens	ones
2	2	5
+ 1	6	6

hundreds	tens	ones
3	6	8
+ 1	1	1

hundreds	tens	ones
2	0	3
+ 2	5	8

3.

hundreds	tens	ones
7	3	9
+ 1	4	2

hundreds	tens	ones
3	6	7
+	1	3

hundreds	tens	ones
5	2	3
+ 1	0	6

PROBLEM SOLVING

Solve.

4. There are 329 cans of peanuts. There are 221 cans of walnuts. How many cans of nuts are there in all?

_____ cans

5. Rick counted 102 boxes of oat cereal. He counted 89 boxes of corn cereal. How many boxes of cereal did he count in all?

_____ boxes

© Houghton Mifflin Harcourt Publishing Company

Adding 3-Digit Numbers

Use place-value models. Add.

1.

hundreds	tens	ones
1		
2	7	3
+ 1	6	4
4	3	7

hundreds	tens	ones
5	6	1
+	1	9

hundreds	tens	ones
2	7	8
+ 2	1	1

2.

hundreds	tens	ones
3	5	4
+ 3	0	6

hundreds	tens	ones
6	7	0
+ 2	4	9

hundreds	tens	ones
4	0	5
+ 5	2	8

3.

834	468	106	333	691
+ 82	+ 426	+ 516	+ 465	+ 118

PROBLEM SOLVING

Solve. Use a calculator.

4. Ian clipped the wool of 348 sheep. Nell clipped 292 sheep. How many sheep did they clip in all?

_____ sheep

5. There are 168 hours in one week. How many hours are in 2 weeks?

_____ hours

© Houghton Mifflin Harcourt Publishing Company

More Adding 3-Digit Numbers

Add.

1.
```
    1
  629          439          432          562          135
+ 154        + 258        + 483        + 396        + 593
-----
  783
```

2.
```
  537          516          608          320          256
+  23        + 133        + 347        + 497        + 316
```

3.
```
  725          154          390          456          708
+ 154        +  29        + 595        + 293        +  58
```

PROBLEM SOLVING

Solve.

4. The supermarket has 134 cans of vegetables and 290 cans of fruit. How many cans are there in all?

_____ cans

5. There are 236 bottles of apple juice and 328 bottles of grape juice. How many bottles are there in all?

_____ bottles

© Houghton Mifflin Harcourt Publishing Company

3-Digit Subtraction: Regroup Tens

Solve. Write the difference.

1.

Hundreds	Tens	Ones
	6	14
7	7	4
− 2	3	6
5	3	8

2.

Hundreds	Tens	Ones
5	5	1
− 1	1	3

3.

Hundreds	Tens	Ones
4	8	9
− 2	7	3

4.

Hundreds	Tens	Ones
7	7	2
− 2	5	4

PROBLEM SOLVING

Solve. Write or draw to explain.

5. There were 985 pencils. Some pencils
were sold. Then there were 559 pencils
left. How many pencils were sold?

_____ pencils

© Houghton Mifflin Harcourt Publishing Company

3-Digit Subtraction: Regroup Hundreds

Solve. Write the difference.

1.

Hundreds	Tens	Ones
6	12	☐
7̸	2̸	7
− 2	5	6
4	7	1

2.

Hundreds	Tens	Ones
☐	☐	☐
9	6	7
− 1	5	3

3.

Hundreds	Tens	Ones
☐	☐	☐
6	3	9
− 4	7	2

4.

Hundreds	Tens	Ones
☐	☐	☐
4	4	8
− 3	6	3

PROBLEM SOLVING

Solve. Write or draw to explain.

5. There were 537 people in the parade. 254 of these people were playing an instrument. How many people were not playing an instrument?

_____ people

© Houghton Mifflin Harcourt Publishing Company

Name _____ Date _____

Exploring 3-Digit Subtraction

Use place-value models.
Find the differences. Trade if you need to.

1.

hundreds	tens	ones
	7	11
2	8̸	1̸
− 1	6	4
1	1	7

hundreds	tens	ones
	☐	☐
6	7	3
− 4	4	9

hundreds	tens	ones
	☐	☐
8	8	7
− 3	2	8

2.

hundreds	tens	ones
	☐	☐
4	5	6
− 1	2	8

hundreds	tens	ones
	☐	☐
4	9	0
− 1	7	2

hundreds	tens	ones
	☐	☐
6	5	4
− 3	3	8

3.

hundreds	tens	ones
	☐	☐
4	2	1
− 2	1	6

hundreds	tens	ones
	☐	☐
3	4	2
−	2	4

hundreds	tens	ones
	☐	☐
5	8	1
− 1	5	9

NUMBER SENSE

Circle your estimate.

4.
```
  500
− 100
```
The difference is < 300.

The difference is > 300.

5.
```
  500
− 300
```
The difference is < 300.

The difference is > 300.

© Houghton Mifflin Harcourt Publishing Company

Understanding 3-Digit Subtraction

Use place-value models.
Find the differences. Trade if you need to.

1.

hundreds	tens	ones
	5	18
7	6	8
− 3	2	9
4	3	9

hundreds	tens	ones
8	5	3
− 4	0	5

hundreds	tens	ones
6	8	2
−	1	7

2.

hundreds	tens	ones
6	3	5
− 1	0	7

hundreds	tens	ones
7	5	4
− 6	2	5

hundreds	tens	ones
8	2	3
− 5	1	2

3.

$$576 - 69 \qquad 472 - 256 \qquad 683 - 244 \qquad 756 - 135 \qquad 470 - 244$$

PROBLEM SOLVING

4. There are 352 monkeys and 218 lions in the park. How many more monkeys are there than lions?

_____ more monkeys

5. There are 250 hippos in the park. 32 hippos are babies. The rest are adults. How many adult hippos are there?

_____ adult hippos

© Houghton Mifflin Harcourt Publishing Company

Subtracting 3-Digit Numbers

Use place-value models. Subtract.

1.

hundreds	tens	ones
4	1	9
− 2	2	5
1	9	4

hundreds	tens	ones
5	7	6
− 1	8	3

hundreds	tens	ones
2	3	5
−	1	8

2.

hundreds	tens	ones
8	2	1
− 5	0	1

hundreds	tens	ones
6	4	2
− 2	7	1

hundreds	tens	ones
7	3	3
− 3	4	3

3.

$$958 - 42$$ $$600 - 200$$ $$313 - 182$$ $$504 - 372$$ $$972 - 656$$

PROBLEM SOLVING

Solve.

4. Use your calculator. Subtract.

$$864 - 519$$

5. The teacher has 442 math books and 327 science books. How many more math books than science books does he have?

_____ more math books

_____ more math books

© Houghton Mifflin Harcourt Publishing Company

Name _____ Date _____

Draw Equal Groups

Work with a friend. Use cubes to show equal groups.
Then draw equal groups of dots on the clown hats.

1. 2 groups of 4

2. 3 groups of 4

3. 3 groups of 2

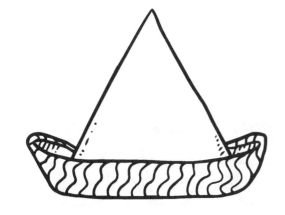

4. 4 groups of 5

NUMBER SENSE

5. Circle the hat that shows equal groups.

141

© Houghton Mifflin Harcourt Publishing Company

Name _____ Date _____

Representing Equal Groups

Write how many groups. Then write the addition sentence.

1.

___2___ groups of 1   _____ groups of 2

___1___ + ___1___ = ___2___   ____ + ____ + ____ = ____

2.

_____ groups of 5   _____ groups of 3

____ + ____ + ____ = ____   ____ + ____ = ____

3.

_____ groups of 2   _____ groups of 4

____ + ____ = ____   ____ + ____ + ____ = ____

REASONING

4. Circle the child who has more shells.

 I collected 4 shells every day for 2 days.

 I collected 2 shells every day for 5 days.

142

© Houghton Mifflin Harcourt Publishing Company

Name _____ Date _____

Repeated Addition

Find the number of shapes in each row.
Complete the addition sentence to find the total.

1.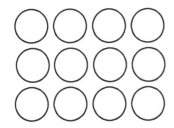

3 rows of __4__

__4__ + __4__ + __4__ = __12__

2.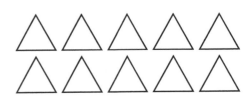

2 rows of ____

____ + ____ = ____

3.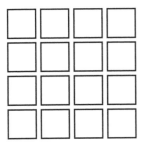

4 rows of ____

____ + ____ + ____ + ____ = ____

4.

4 rows of ____

____ + ____ + ____ + ____ = ____

PROBLEM SOLVING

Solve. Write or draw to explain.

5. A classroom has 3 rows of desks.
There are 5 desks in each row.
How many desks are there altogether?

_____ desks

© Houghton Mifflin Harcourt Publishing Company

Unit 13
Core Skills Math, Grade 2

Exploring Addition and Multiplication

Use counters to help you find the totals.

1. 3
  + 3

2. 5
    5
  + 5

3. 2
    2
  + 2

2 threes = _____   3 fives = _____   3 twos = _____

Draw a picture for each number sentence. Solve.

4. 4
    4
  + 4

5. 7
    7
  + 7

3 fours = _____   3 sevens = _____

VISUAL THINKING

6. Circle the addition sentence
   and the multiplication sentence
   that tell about the picture.

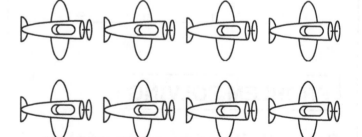

2 + 4 = 6   4 + 4 = 8   3 + 3 = 6

2 threes = 6   1 two and 1 four = 6   2 fours = 8

144

© Houghton Mifflin Harcourt Publishing Company

Multiplication Sentences

Use the number line. Write the addition sentence.
Then write the multiplication sentence.

1.

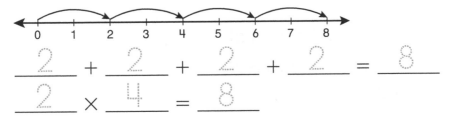

__2__ + __2__ + __2__ + __2__ = __8__

__2__ × __4__ = __8__

2.

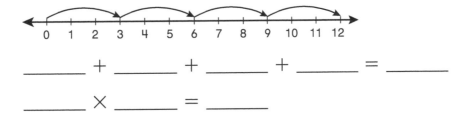

_____ + _____ + _____ + _____ = _____

_____ × _____ = _____

3.

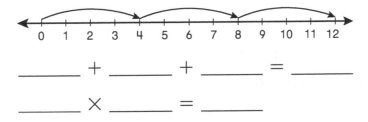

_____ + _____ + _____ = _____

_____ × _____ = _____

PROBLEM SOLVING

Show the problem on the number line.
Write the addition sentence and the multiplication sentence.

4. Cass has 5 dolls from each country her
uncle has visited. He has been to 4 countries.
How many dolls does Cass have from her uncle?

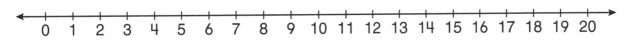

_____ + _____ + _____ + _____ = _____

_____ × _____ = _____

© Houghton Mifflin Harcourt Publishing Company

Name _____ Date _____

Problem Solving

| EQUAL GROUPS |

Act out the problem. Draw to show what you did.

1. Mr. Anderson has 4 plates of crackers. There are 5 crackers on each plate. How many crackers are there in all?

_____ crackers

2. Ms. Trane puts some stickers in 3 rows. There are 2 stickers in each row. How many stickers does Ms. Trane have?

_____ stickers

3. There are 5 books in each box. How many books are in 5 boxes?

_____ books

© Houghton Mifflin Harcourt Publishing Company

Answer Key

Page 1

1. 9
2. 8
3. 9
4. 8
5. 7
6. 8
7. 6
8. 6
9. 9 + 5

Page 2

1. 8, 8, 10, 10, 10, 10
2. 8, 10, 13, 5, 8, 10
3. 6, 12, 9, 4, 9, 9
4. Circle middle train.
5. Circle top train.

Page 3

1. 3 + 6 = 9
2. 8 + 2 = 10
3. 0 + 3 = 3
4. 1 + 6 = 7
5. 6 + 3 = 9
6. 5 + 4 = 9
7. 4 + 5 = 9; 9

Page 4

1. 10, 7, 7, 11, 8, 11
2. 10, 8, 8, 6, 10, 9
3. 4, 5, 3, 12, 10, 5
4. 5, 6, 7, 6, 9, 9
5. 4
6. 7

Page 5

1. circle 5, 7; circle 8, 9; circle 5, 8; circle 6, 7; circle 7, 9; circle 7, 10
2. circle 4, 5; circle 4, 7; circle 4, 6; circle 9, 10; circle 6, 8; circle 8, 10
3. circle 9, 11; circle 7, 8; circle 8, 11; circle 6, 9; circle 5, 8; circle 4, 6
4. circle 9, 12; circle 7, 10; circle 6, 9; circle 8, 10; circle 5, 6; circle 3, 4
5. 9
6. 16

Page 6

1. 0, 5, 0
2. 6, 0, 0
3. 4, 0, 8
4. 0, 7, 1
5. 0, 3, 0, 9, 0
6. Possible answer: 7 − 7 = 0

Page 7

1. 5 − 3 = 2
2. 8 − 3 = 5
3. 6 − 2 = 4
4. 5 − 2 = 3
5. Circle first number line.

Page 8

1. 4, 7, 4, 2, 8
2. 6, 2, 6, 1, 9, 3
3. 7, 5, 8, 1, 5, 3
4. 4 − 2 = 2; 2
5. 6 − 1 = 5; 5

Page 9

1. 8
2. 5
3. 6
4. 7
5. 7, 8, 7, 6, 6, 9
6. 0
7. 0

Page 10

Circle the bottom numbers for 1–4.

1. 2, 1, 1, 3, 2, 1
2. 3, 1, 2, 3, 1, 3
3. 2, 2, 1, 1, 3, 2
4. 3, 1, 2, 2, 2, 3
5. 8

Page 11

Order may vary in 1–4.

1. 7 + 3 = 10; 3 + 7 = 10; 10 − 7 = 3; 10 − 3 = 7
2. 1 + 7 = 8; 7 + 1 = 8; 8 − 1 = 7; 8 − 7 = 1
3. 6 + 1 = 7; 1 + 6 = 7; 7 − 6 = 1; 7 − 1 = 6
4. 4 + 2 = 6; 2 + 4 = 6; 6 − 4 = 2; 6 − 2 = 4
5. 2

Page 12

1. 9 − 2 = 7; 7
2. 5 + 5 = 10; 10
3. 10 − 4 = 6; 6
4. 4 + 4 = 8 or 8 − 4 = 4

Page 13

1. 2, 14, 4, 16, 8
2. 0, 6, 12, 18, 10
3. 5, 10, 8, 9, 6, 10;
Circle 4 + 4, 3 + 3, 5 + 5.
4. 4
5. 6

Page 14

1. Circle 4 + 5, 3 + 4, 6 + 5; 8, 9, 7, 6, 11, 10
2. Circle 6 + 7, 2 + 3, 9 + 8; 13, 12, 4, 5, 16, 17
3. 7, red; 6, blue; 4, blue; 15, red; 13, red; 8, blue
4. Circle the second and fourth pictures.

Page 15

1. 14, 14
2. 12, 12
3. 17, 17
4. 13, 15, 16, 17, 12
5. Circle 9 + 2 and 10 + 1.
6. Circle 10 + 3 and 9 + 4.

Page 16

1. 13, 12, 12, 13, 15, 13
2. 11, 14, 14, 15, 11, 13
3. 11, 12, 12, 16, 14, 14
4. 7 − 5 = 2; 2
5. 6 + 7 = 13; 13

Page 17

1. 11, 12, 11, 13, 14
2. 17, 17, 14, 17, 15, 13
3. 16, 15, 16, 19, 18, 14
4. 13, circle
5. 7
6. 13, circle
7. 12, circle
8. 8

Page 18

Last row of addends will vary for 1–4.

1. 9, 14; 8, 14; 7, 14; 4, 10, 14

© Houghton Mifflin Harcourt Publishing Company

2. 9, 13; 8, 13; 7, 13; 7, 6, 13
3. 9, 12; 8, 12; 7, 12; 6, 6, 12
4. 9, 11; 8, 11; 7, 11; 5, 6, 11
5. 3 + 7, 2 + 7

Page 19

1. 13, 14, 12, 13, 17, 12
2. 14, 11, 14, 14, 15, 13
3. 12, 18, 11, 13, 16, 12
4. 17, 11, 12, 11, 12, 11
5. 11 − 8 = 3; 3
6. 5 + 8 = 13; 13

Page 20

1. 12, 6
2. 10, 5
3. 18, 9
4. 4, 2
5. 6, 3
6. 14, 7
7. 8, 4
8. 16, 8
9. 6 + 6 = 12; 12
10. 12 − 6 = 6; 6

Page 21

Check puzzle answers.
1. 9
2. 13
3. 6
4. 13

Page 22

1. 9, 7, 8; 6, 9, 8; 7, 9, 8; 8, 6, 2
2. 8, 4, 6; 1, 6, 9; 6, 9, 2; 9, 6, 8
3. 4, 9, 3; 5, 3, 7; 2, 8, 7; 8, 7, 3
4. 6 + 7 = 13; 13
5. 12 − 3 = 9; 9

Page 23

1. 7, 15, 14, 15, 8; Circle 7 + 7 = 14.
2. 16, 16, 7, 7, 18; Circle 9 + 9 = 18.
3. 8, 9, 17, 9, 8; Circle 16 − 8 = 8.
4. 6, 6, 8, 14, 14; Circle 15 − 9 = 6.
5. 6 + 6 = 12; 12 − 6 = 6

Page 24

1. 16, 9, 16
2. 13, 5, 13
3. 11, 6, 11
4. 14, 9, 11, 18, 7, 7
5. 8, 8, 13, 15, 5, 12
6. 5 + 5 = 10; 10
7. 5 + 6 = 11; 11

Page 25

1. 15; Yes; 1, 5
2. 9; No; 0, 9
3. 13; Yes; 1, 3
4. 12; Yes; 1, 2
5. 1 ten 3 ones; 13 ones

Page 26

1. Circle 2 groups of 10; 2, 3; 23
2. Circle 3 groups of 10; 3, 2; 32
3. Circle 4 groups of 10; 4, 8; 48
4. Circle 4 groups of 10; 4, 1; 41
5. Circle 2 groups of 10; 2, 9; 29
6. Circle 2 groups of 10; 2, 6; 26
7. Circle first group; the group is easier to count because the shapes are in rows..

Page 27

1. 34, 43, 40
2. 32, 14, 4
3. 21, 24, 30
4. 25
5. 74

Page 28

1. 85, 62
2. 87
3. 63
4. 59
5. 86
6. 92, 65, 83
7. 76, 48, 93
8. fewer than 30

Page 29

Possible answers are given for 1–10.
1. 3, 2
2. 41
3. ninety-five
4. 83
5. 5, 7
6. 70 + 2
7. 64
8. 48
9. 20 + 8
10. 8, 0
11. 40 + 3

Page 30

1–6. Circle 4, 2, 8; draw X on 5, 1, 11. Check coloring.
7. Circle 12, 6, 18, 22. Draw X on 3, 7, 9, 13, 17.

8. Even Number

Page 31

Check coloring for 1–6.
1. odd
2. even
3. odd
4. odd
5. odd
6. even
7. 9 sheep and 10 cows

Page 32

Check coloring for 1–6.
1. 8 = 4 + 4
2. 18 = 9 + 9
3. 10 = 5 + 5
4. 14 = 7 + 7
5. 20 = 10 + 10
6. 12 = 6 + 6
7. 8

Page 33

1. 5, 10, 15, 16; 16
2. 10, 20, 30, 31; 31
3. 10, 15, 20, 25, 26; 26
4. 10, 20, 30, 40, 45, 46; 46
5. 5¢, 5¢, 5¢
6. 10¢, 10¢, 10¢, 10¢

Page 34

1. 25, 35, 40, 41; 41
2. 25, 30, 35, 36, 37; 37
3. 25, 35, 45, 50, 55; 55
4. 25, 35, 40, 41, 42, 43; 43
5. 36
6. 7

Page 35

1. 31, 25, 36; circle 36
2. 35, 27, 25; circle 35
3. 40, 30, 41; circle 41
4. Tina

Page 36

1. 27
2. 13
3. 17
4. 40
5. 16
6. 55
7. Stories will vary.

© Houghton Mifflin Harcourt Publishing Company

Page 37

1. 72
2. 76
3. 62
4. 70
5. 89
6. 81
7. Circle first belt.

Page 38

Check work for 1–3.
4. Circle second group.

Page 39

Check drawings for 1–3.
1. 55
2. 80
3. 40
4. 51¢

Page 40

Answers will vary for 1–5.
6. Circle second and third groups.

Page 41

1. dollar, 5 pennies
2. dollar, quarter, 3 nickels
3. dollar, nickel, dime, 2 pennies
4. dollar, half dollar, 4 dimes, nickel
5. $1.15; circle $1.25
6. Yes

Page 42

1. 60, 70; 12
2. 30, 35; 7
3. 54, 55, 65; 13
4. 25¢, 1¢

Page 43

1. 95, Yes
2. 80, No
3. 81, No
4. 60, Yes
5. more than 50¢

Page 44

1. $30 + 50 = 80$; 80
2. $25 + 25 = 50$; 50
3. cube
4. No

Page 45

1. $75 - 50 = 25$; 25
2. $50 - 40 = 10$; 10
3. $32 + 5 = 37$; 37
4. $37 - 27 = 10$; 10
5. Answers will vary.

Page 46

1. 3:00
2. 10:30
3. 4:00
4. 9:00
5. 12:30
6. 9:30
7. Draw minute hand to 12, hour hand to 4.

Page 47

1. 5:15, 7:00, 10:45
2. 11:45, 6:30, 8:15
3. 3:45, 5:30, 9:15
4. 8:45
5. 2:30

Page 48

1. 8:15
2. 2:40
3. 5:55
4. 6:10
5. 3:35
6. 11:20
7. Draw minute hand to 9; 4:45

Page 49

Check drawings for 1–3.
1. 1 egg, 2 eggs, 3 eggs, 4 eggs
2. 5 eggs, 6 eggs, 7 eggs, 8 eggs
3. 9 eggs, 10 eggs, 11 eggs, 12 eggs
4. Circle second glass.

Page 50

Check drawings for 1–6.
1. Draw minute hand to 3; 7:15
2. Draw minute hand to 6; 3:30
3. Draw minute hand to 10; 1:50
4. Draw minute hand to 3; 11:15
5. Draw minute hand to 3; 8:15
6. Draw minute hand to 1; 6:05
7. Draw minute hand to 6.

Page 51

1. 4:40, P.M.
2. 7:30, A.M.
3. 8:15, P.M.
4. 8:20, P.M.
5. 7:00 A.M.; 8:30 A.M.; 3:15 P.M.

Page 52

1. 11, Yes, 2, 1
2. 12, Yes, 4, 2
3. 9, No, 6, 9
4. 18, Yes, 3, 8
5. 13, Yes, 5, 3
6. 17, 17

Page 53

Check work for 1–4. Possible answers are given.
1. $12 + 40 = 52$
2. $21 + 50 = 71$
3. $40 + 24 = 64$
4. $30 + 44 = 74$ or $24 + 50 = 74$
5. 52

Page 54

1. 7 tens 2 ones; 72
2. 8 tens 3 ones; 83
3. 7 tens 6 ones; 76
4. 9 tens 0 ones; 90
5. 9 tens 4 ones; 94
6. 5 tens 5 ones; 55
7. 81

Page 55

1. $10 + 8$; $20 + 1$; $30 + 9 = 39$
2. $30 + 3$; $40 + 9$; $70 + 12 = 82$
3. $70 + 2$; $10 + 8$; $80 + 10 = 90$
4. 46

Page 56

Check drawings for 1–4.
1. 55
2. 84
3. 79
4. 91
5. 62; Explanations will vary.

Page 57

1. 33, 50, 23, 30
2. 31, 62, 31, 74
3. 53, 42, 62, 34
4. less than 80
5. greater than 80

149

© Houghton Mifflin Harcourt Publishing Company

Page 58

1. 61, 46, 76, 74
2. 46, 51, 53, 60
3. 44
4. 8, 1

Page 59

1. 76, 76, 68, 73, 71, 47
2. 99, 96, 40, 62, 97, 81
3. 76, 80, 22, 45, 83, 93
4. Theo

Page 60

1. 47, 83, 85, 79, 63, 65
2. 52, 44, 82, 76, 51, 59
3. 62, 62, 55, 71, 84, 93
4. 55; $16 + 39 = 55$

Page 61

1. about 60
2. about 80
3. about 70
4. about 90

Page 62

1. 23
2. Circle "The game has 35 red cards."; 60
3. the first number

Page 63

1. 20, 20, 40, 80; 40, 20, 30, 90; 20, 20, 30, 70
2. 68, 62, 99, 82, 83, 68
3. 3 quarters; $25 + 25 + 25 = 75$

Page 64

1. 76
2. 177
3. 189
4. 198
5. 95
6. 148
7. 58

Page 65

1. Yes; 2 tens 9 ones
2. Yes; 3 tens 5 ones
3. Yes; 1 ten 3 ones
4. No; 3 tens 1 one
5. Yes; 4 tens 3 ones
6. No; 1 ten 0 ones
7. less than 40

Page 66

1. 36, 31, 22, 41
2. 29, 17, 17, 39
3. 24, 67, 59, 49
4. $59 - 9 = 50$; 50
5. $23 - 8 = 15$; 15

Page 67

1. 55, No; 41, No; 23, Yes
2. 29, Yes; 28, Yes; 75; Yes
3. 39, Yes; 26, Yes; 91, No
4. 3, 17

Page 68

Check drawings for 1–4.
1. 2 tens 6 ones; 26
2. 3 tens 8 ones; 38
3. 2 tens 9 ones; 29
4. 3 tens 5 ones; 35
5. 37

Page 69

1. 26, Yes; 12, No; 69, Yes; 23, No
2. 48, Yes; 17, Yes; 72, No; 57, Yes
3. 37, Yes; 79, Yes; 81, No; 72, No
4. $84 - 25 = 59$; 59
5. $57 - 25 = 32$; 3, 2

Page 70

1. 26, I; 12, 69, 23, SAW; 48, 26, 37, 79, 12, LIONS; 69, 62, AT; 62, 31, 72, THE; 52, 37, 37, ZOO
2. Answers will vary.

Page 71

1. 55, $55 + 12 = 67$;
   39, $39 + 48 = 87$;
   35, $35 + 57 = 92$
2. 6, $6 + 77 = 83$;
   15, $15 + 30 = 45$;
   33, $33 + 21 = 54$
3. 29, $29 + 32 = 61$;
   52, $52 + 28 = 80$;
   17, $17 + 55 = 72$
4. $30 - 19 = 11$; 11
5. $27 + 15 = 42$; 42

Page 72

1. 16
2. 81
3. 24
4. about 40

Page 73

Check work. Left side of tugboat (additions): 87, 88, 89, 90, 91, 92, 93, 94, 95, 96; Right side of tugboat (subtractions): 12, 13, 14, 15, 16, 17, 18, 19, 20, 21

Story Corner answers will vary.

Page 74

1. 4 spaceships
2. 32 pennies
3. 8 years old
4. 38 children
5. 30 trips

Page 75

1. $92 - 56 = 36$; 36
2. $43 + 36 = 79$; 79
3. $56 + 43 = 99$; 99
4. $79 - 36 = 43$; 43
5. $87 - 58 = 29$; 29
6. $79 - 47 = 32$; 32

Page 76

1. 39; 77, 39, 77
2. 48; 63, 48, 63
3. 30

Page 77

1. Check coloring.
2. 2, 5, 4
3. Check coloring.
4. 5, 2, 3
5. circle

Page 78

Check drawings for 1–4.
5. Answers will vary.

Page 79

1. Circle second and fourth figures.
2. Circle first and third figures.
3. Circle second and fourth figures.
4. octagon
5. triangle

Page 80

Check drawings for 1–7.

150

© Houghton Mifflin Harcourt Publishing Company

Page 81

1. Circle third figure.
2. Circle third and fourth figures.
3. Circle first and second figures.
4. closed figure, polygon
5. Yes
6. No

Page 82

Guesses will vary for 1–3.
1. 10
2. 6
3. 6

Page 83

1. 2, 3; 6
2. 1, 2; 2
3. 9; 3, 3, 9

Page 84

1. 8, 3, 2, 0
2. 4, 6, 2, 3
3. 2, 10, 0, 8
4. 6, 4, 5, 7
5. Check drawings.

Page 85

Check drawings for 1–3.

Page 86

Check coloring for 1–3.
4. No

Page 87

1. 1, 2, 3
2. 5, 6, 3
3. $\frac{2}{8}, \frac{2}{4}, \frac{3}{10}$
4. $\frac{4}{5}, \frac{3}{8}, \frac{2}{3}$
5. $\frac{1}{2}, \frac{2}{4}$

Page 88

Check work for 1–3.
4. shorter than 1 foot
5. longer than 1 foot

Page 89

Measurements will vary for 1–3.
1. 7 inches
2. 2 inches
3. 5 inches
4. 1 inch

Page 90

1. 1 inch
2. 3 inches
3. 6 inches
Check lines for 4–6.
7. Answers will vary.
8. 10 inches

Page 91

Answers will vary for 1–2. Check work.
3. yardstick; Check explanations.

Page 92

Answers will vary for 1–3. Check work.
4. Jake; Feet are longer than inches.

Page 93

1. about 1 foot
2. 100 yards
3. 10 yards
4. 2 miles
5. 2 feet
6. 20 miles
7. 36
8. 36

Page 94

Check drawings for 1–3.
4. Accept reasonable answers.
5. 10

Page 95

Check drawings for 1–4.
5. 20

Page 96

1. 8 cm
2. 5 cm
Check drawings for 3–5.
Accept reasonable answers for 6–7.

Page 97

1. 11, 8; 11 − 8 = 3; 3
2. 6, 10; 10 − 6 = 4; 4
3. 13; Check explanations.

Page 98

Check work for 1–3.
4. meters; Meters are longer than centimeters.

Page 99

1. 3 meters
2. 1 meter
3. less than 1 meter
4. more than 1 meter
5. more than 1 kilometer
6. less than 1 kilometer
7. 24
8. 65

Page 100

Accept reasonable answers for 1–5.
6. inches
7. Suzi

Page 101

Check drawings for 1–2.
1. 23 − 7 = ■; 16
2. 11 + 7 = ■; 18

Page 102

Answers will vary for 1–2.
3. Check drawings.

Page 103

Answers will vary for 1–6, but should match the data in the tally chart.

Page 104

Table: 26, 17, 8, 13
1. 8
2. 30
3. swimming
4. Answers will vary.

Page 105

1. 2, 4, 5, 7
2. 10, 15, 20
3. 20
4. 15

Page 106

1. 5
2. soccer
3. 2
4. football
5. 10
6. 8

Page 107

Answers will vary for 1–2.
Graph should match table.
3. shortest bar

© Houghton Mifflin Harcourt Publishing Company

Page 108

1. Check bar graph, title, and labels. The number decreased each month.
2. 15
3. 2
4. April, May

Page 109

1. 12
2. 16
3. C
4. 28
5. No
6. 8 children

Page 110

1. 9
2. 2
3. 4
4. 15
5. 2

Page 111

1. Thursday
2. 20
3. 6 faces; 2 faces; 4 faces
4. Possible answer: Lunch Choices
5. 5; Explanations will vary.

Page 112

1. 200
2. 400
3. 600
4. 800
5. 900
6. 700
7. 500
8. 300
9. 100
10. 400
11. 400

Page 113

1. 40, 4, 400
2. 60, 6, 600
3. 90, 9, 900
4. 300; Check work.

Page 114

1. 3, 2, 4; 324
2. 5, 6, 1; 561
3. 4, 3, 5; 435
4. 8
5. 40
6. 200
7. 3

Page 115

1. 6, 4, 0; 6, 5, 0; 660, 6, 6, 0; 670, 6, 7, 0; 680, 6, 8, 0; 690, 6, 9, 0
2. 3, 0, 0; 400, 4, 0, 0; 500, 5, 0, 0; 600, 6, 0, 0; 700, 7, 0, 0; 800, 8, 0, 0
3. Circle 17 tens and 1 hundred and 7 tens

Page 116

1. 5, 4, 3; 543
2. 6, 8, 2; 682
3. 4, 8, 7; 487
4. 3, 8, 5; 385
5. 2, 6, 1; 261
6. 1, 9, 0; 190
7. 183
8. 831

Page 117

1. 7, 2, 8, 700, 20, 8; 2, 7, 8, 200, 70, 8
2. 5, 1, 6, 500, 10, 6; 6, 5, 1, 600, 50, 1
3. 4, 3, 7, 400, 30, 7; 3, 4, 7, 300, 40, 7
4. 907
5. 620

Page 118

1. 487
2. 552
3. 807
4. 611
5. **Across:**
   1. 200
   2. 450
   4. 9
   5. 718
   6. 456
   9. 789
   11. 573
   13. 500
   14. 16
   15. 998
   Down:
   1. 294
   2. 417
   3. 588
   7. 555
   8. 670
   10. 906
   12. 309
   14. 18
6. 340

Page 119

1. 232
2. 544
3. 158
4. 950
5. 420
6. 678
7. three hundred seventeen
8. four hundred fifty-seven
9. 626

Page 120

Answers may vary. Check drawings.
1. 2 hundreds 5 tens 1 one; 200 + 50 + 1; 251
2. 3 hundreds 1 ten 2 ones; 300 + 10 + 2; 312
3. 2 hundreds 0 tens 7 ones; 200 + 0 + 7; 207

Possible answers given for 4–5.
4. 237
5. 800 + 90 + 5

152

Page 121

1. Circle 314; 431
2. Circle 453; 543
3. Circle 203; 302
4. 330; circle 303
5. Circle 167, 478, 823, 323, 109

Page 122

1. $<$, $<$, $<$
2. $>$, $<$, $>$
3. $>$, $<$, $>$
4. $<$, $>$, $>$
5. $<$, $>$, $>$
6. 27, 56, 98, 109, 129
7. 82, 208, 280, 802, 820

Page 123

Check drawings for 1–4.
1. Lauryn
2. Nick
3. more white keys
4. fewer in the bag

Page 124

1. 723
2. 109
3. 475
4. 316
5. 579
6. 740
7. 485
8. 610
9. 34, 234; 356, 556; 772, 972; 407, 607
10. 4
11. 30

Page 125

1. 60, 61, 62, 63, 64
2. 55, 60, 65, 70, 75
3. 30, 35, 40, 45, 50
4. 30, 40, 50, 60, 70, 80
5. 84, 83, 82
6. 10, 15, 20, 25, 30

Page 126

1. 425, 430, 435, 440
2. 685, 690, 695, 700, 705
3. 230, 240, 250, 260, 270
4. 860, 870, 880, 890, 900
5. 500, 600, 700, 800, 900
6. 951, 950, 949, 948, 947
7. 110, 120, 130, 140, 150

Page 127

1. 461
2. 760
3. 467
4. 795
5. 802
6. 643
7. 228
8. 479
9. 224
10. 819
11. 118

Page 128

1. 272, 282
2. 585, 685
3. 828, 928
4. 694, 704
5. 733, 833
6. 471, 501

Page 129

1. 6
2. 400
3. 9
4. 80
5. 70
6. 32
7. 4, 5, 0; $400 + 50 + 0$
8. 5, 0, 3; $500 + 0 + 3$
9. 6, 8, 1; $600 + 80 + 1$
10. 500, 600, 700
11. 800, 810, 820
12. 392, 402, 412

Page 130

Check drawings for 1–3.
1. 3 hundreds 5 tens 7 ones; 357
2. 4 hundreds 6 tens 9 ones; 469
3. 579

Page 131

1. $500 + 10 + 8$; $200 + 20 + 1$; $700 + 30 + 9$; 739
2. $400 + 30 + 8$; $100 + 40 + 2$; $500 + 70 + 10$; 580
3. $300 + 20 + 4$; $200 + 30 + 9$; $500 + 50 + 13$; 563
4. 270; Check drawings.

Page 132

1. 481, 399, 770
2. 732, 598, 873
3. The sum is > 500.
4. The sum is < 900.

Page 133

1. 739, 545, 564
2. 391, 479, 461
3. 881, 380, 629
4. 550
5. 191

Page 134

1. 437, 580, 489
2. 660, 919, 933
3. 916, 894, 622, 798, 809
4. 640
5. 336

Page 135

1. 783, 697, 915, 958, 728
2. 560, 649, 955, 817, 572
3. 879, 183, 985, 749, 766
4. 424
5. 564

Page 136

1. 538
2. 438
3. 216
4. 518
5. 426

Page 137

1. 471
2. 814
3. 167
4. 85
5. 283

Page 138

1. 117, 224, 559
2. 328, 318, 316
3. 205, 318, 422
4. The difference is > 300.
5. The difference is < 300.

Page 139

1. 439, 448, 665
2. 528, 129, 311
3. 507, 216, 439, 621, 226
4. 134
5. 218

153

Page 140

1. 194, 393, 217
2. 320, 371, 390
3. 916, 400, 131, 132, 316
4. 345
5. 115

Page 141

Check drawings for 1–4.

5. Circle first hat.

Page 142

1. 2, 1 + 1 = 2; 3, 2 + 2 + 2 = 6
2. 3, 5 + 5 + 5 = 15; 2, 3 + 3 = 6
3. 2, 2 + 2 = 4; 3, 4 + 4 + 4 = 12
4. Circle second child.

Page 143

1. 4; 4 + 4 + 4 = 12
2. 5; 5 + 5 = 10
3. 4; 4 + 4 + 4 + 4 = 16
4. 5; 5 + 5 + 5 + 5 = 20
5. 15

Page 144

1. 6, 6
2. 15, 15
3. 6, 6

Check drawings for 4–5.

4. 12, 12
5. 21, 21
6. 4 + 4 = 8; 2 fours = 8

Page 145

1. 2 + 2 + 2 + 2 = 8; 2 × 4 = 8
2. 3 + 3 + 3 + 3 = 12; 3 × 4 = 12
3. 4 + 4 + 4 = 12; 4 × 3 = 12
4. Check drawing. 5 + 5 + 5 + 5 = 20; 5 × 4 = 20

Page 146

1. 20
2. 6
3. 25

154

© Houghton Mifflin Harcourt Publishing Company

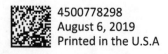
4500778298
August 6, 2019
Printed in the U.S.A